N

NEW SIBERIAN ISLANDS

Yakutia

TED SOCIALIST REPUBLIC

KAMCHATKA

PACIFIC OCEAN

SEA OF OKHOTSK

KURIL ISLANDS

SAKHALIN

Buriat Mongolia

LAKE BAIKAL

Tuva

CHINA

MONGOLIA

JAPAN

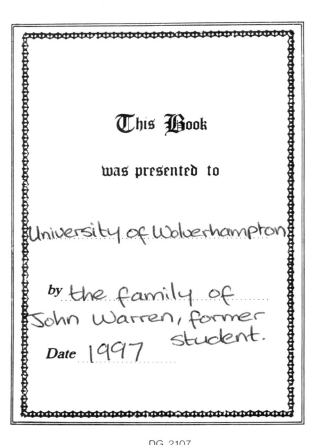

This Book

was presented to

University of Wolverhampton,

by the family of
John Warren, former
student.

Date 1997

DG 2107

SOVIET UNION

Originated and developed by:
Nebojša-Bato TOMAŠEVIĆ

Text by:
PLANETA

Designed by:
Miodrag VARTABEDIJAN

Bracken Books
London

A Motovun Group Book

Originated and developed by:
Nebojša-Bato TOMAŠEVIĆ

Designed by:
Miodrag VARTABEDIJAN

© *World copyright 1989:*
PLANETA, Moscow
JUGOSLAVIAPUBLIC, Belgrade
JUGOSLOVENSKA REVIJA, Belgrade

Directors and Editors-in-Chief:
Vladimir G. SEREDIN
Dragoljub ĐORĐEVIĆ
Rajko BOBOT

Edition editors:
Tamara F. TKACHENKO
Jelena MILOSAVLJEVIĆ
Vlatka RUBINJONI-STRUGAR

Text by
PLANETA

Edited by
Aleksandar NOVAČIĆ

Translator
Una TOMAŠEVIĆ

English language editor
Madge PHILLIPS

Lay out and drawings by
Semion S. VEHOVSKI

Photographs by
PLANETA Photography Service

Additional photographs by
Dragoljub ZAMUROVIĆ
12, 13, 14, 15, 16, 17, 19, 20, 23

First published in the United Kingdom by
BRACKEN BOOKS
an imprint of Bestseller Publications Ltd.
Princess House, 50 Eastcastle Street
London W1N 7AP, England

ISBN 1 85170 270 9

Printed and bound in Yugoslavia by
GORENJSKI TISK, Kranj 1989

Contents

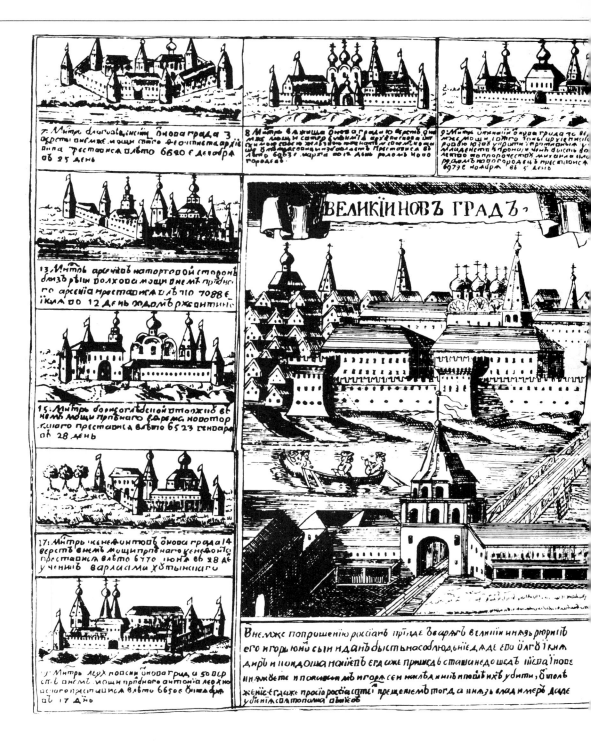

*I*n other countries, the Soviet Union is often referred to as Russia, which is only a part of the Union of Soviet Socialist Republics, albeit the largest. The USSR today consists of fifteen federal republics, twenty autonomous republics, eight autonomous provinces and ten autonomous districts. Even Russia itself is a federation of a number of autonomous republics and districts.

Such a division reflects, in fact, the Soviet Union's history. In ancient times, many large and independent states existed on its present territory. Some of them acquired their glory by conquest, such as the empire of the Uzbek Tamerlane, who ruled the lands from the Bosphorus to China. Others, like medieval Georgia and Armenia, attained renown through their poets, artists and scholars.

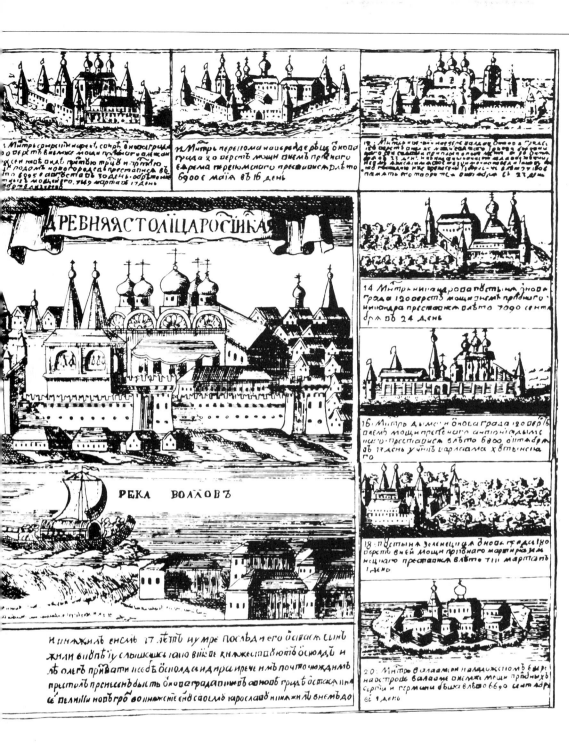

Novgorod, one of the oldest Russian towns, was the second most important town of Kievan Rus as early as the tenth century. Built on the banks of the Volkhova river, it was a main stop of the trade route which connected the north of Europe to Greece and the Black Sea. It was called Great Novgorod for its beauty and magnificent churches.

Not until after the October Revolution, more precisely in 1922, were they all united in the single state of the Soviet Union.

The past has left the present-day USSR a heritage of diverse religious beliefs, customs and traditions. Polytheism, and then Christianity and Islam, exerted strong influences on the development of human thought in old Russia and the Ukraine, as well as in Uzbekistan, Azerbaijan and other Central Asian republics.

In size, the Soviet Union is the largest country in the world. Its 22.4 million square kilometers comprise one sixth of the Earth's total land mass. Three-quarters of Soviet territory is in Asia, and the remaining quarter in Europe. As regards population, it is third, after China and India.

The territorial, climatic and even time differences within the

Soviet Union are enormous. Its northernmost and southernmost points are over five thousand kilometers apart, while the distance is twice as great between its farthest eastern and western points. The waves of twelve seas and three oceans break on its shores. The country has as many as eleven time zones: while Moscow is celebrating the arrival of the New Year, in the Far East a new day has already dawned. So vast are the Soviet lands.

In these expanses greater and lesser cultures and civilizations were created and vanished over thousands of years. Some of them left a strong imprint on their age, some are still present today, others have disappeared leaving scarcely a trace, so that more is guessed than known about where and how they were formed, and why they died out.

This historical and civilizational diversity is a key to understanding the Soviet Union, inhabited by over 260 million people and over 100 different nations.

This monograph is a journey into the history of this great land, whose peoples in the past not only lived in separate states that were frequently at war, but were sometimes ignorant of each other's existence. From the first known human settlement on the territory of the Soviet Union, at Satani Dar in Armenia, over half a million years ago, down to the present day, when certain national groups, such as the Chukchas in the Far North, are only just acquiring literacy and other national attributes, so many years and events have passed that it is impossible to summarize them in a single book. All this has left its mark, to a greater or lesser extent, on the present-day Union of Soviet Socialist Republics.

It is impossible to understand this land without looking into the past of its peoples and the many cultures which flourished and decayed on its territory, into the customs and traditions of its inhabitants, into the religious, scientific and artistic views they held, into the historical ambitions and goals they cherished. This monograph attempts to answer some of these questions.

1. View of Moscow from the Bolshoi Theater, with Karl Marx Square in the foreground, and the Kremlin with the illuminated Spasskaya gate-tower in the distance. The red star, made of rubies, on its top 'shines' day and night.

2. The golden domes of Moscow. The summits of the Cathedral of the Annunciation, the Court church, and Ivan the Great's bell-tower, form a harmonious entity. The lavishly decorated Russian Orthodox churches have great intrinsic as well as spiritual and artistic value: the domes of many important churches are covered with a thin layer of gold. By a special procedure, the gold was spread on sheets of special paper, which were then simply laid against the metal dome and 'stuck' to the surface without any chemical or other adhesive means (pp. 10—11).

3. Moscow, the capital of Russia and the USSR, has a long and tumultuous history. The existence of a settlement here on the Moskva river is first recorded in a document from 1147. The Muscovite principality led the struggle for liberation from the Mongols and the unification of all Russians. Today the city has eight million inhabitants, a developed infrastructure and industry, and all the advantages and drawbacks of any metropolis (pp. 12—13).

9

9. The Pokrovski Sobor, better known as the Cathedral of St Basil the Blessed, stands on the Red Square. One of the landmarks of Moscow, it was raised in 1555 by the masterbuilders Barma and Postnik. Its nine quite different domes make this a unique architectural ensemble.

10.   'The Farewell to the Russian
Winter' is a traditional popular
festivity. With music and
performances by folklore societies,
the celebration is carried to parks and
squares throughout the city. 'Russian
Winter' also attracts numerous tourists
from all over the world.

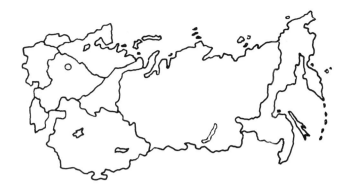

The Heart of Russia
Moscow

The history of Moscow's Kremlin reaches deep into the past: the earliest mention of Moscow (Moskva) dates back over eight hundred years.

In 1147, the son of Vladimir Monomakh, Prince Yuri of Suzdal, later named Dolgoruki ('Long Arm') because of his ambition to conquer distant towns, invited his ally and relative, Prince Svyatoslav of Novgorod: "Come to me, brother, to Moscow." There, in Moscow, Yuri treated his guest to a 'lavish feast'. The date of the first historical mention of Moscow, 1147, has been taken as the year of the city's foundation.

The Lavrentian Chronicle records that the first wooden stockade around the Kremlin (*Kreml* = fortress) was raised in 1156.

Archeological excavations, however, have revealed that this slightly elevated site surrounded by rivers — the Neglina, the Yauza and the largest one later to be called the Moskva — was inhabited as far back as five or six thousand years ago. It was not until the tenth century, however, that Slav colonization of this territory began; two of the fourteen East Slav tribes — the Vyatichi and the Krivichi — are considered its first inhabitants.

Moscow, or Muscovy as it used to be called in the West, lay in a fertile plain, where agriculture was developed and the rivers provided good trading connections with other regions. Like the whole of Russia, the city was exposed to attacks from neighboring states, and from the thirteenth century to the onslaught of the Mongols, in particular, who had formed a powerful state in central Asia (1206), whence they launched their conquest of western lands. At that time Russia was not yet united and frequent internal quarrels among the individual princes only served to weaken its defenses. It is recorded that Moscow was first burnt down in 1237, when it was taken by Mongol-Tartar tribes. The chronicler records that, apart from the 'citadel' all the 'monasteries and villages' were also burnt, from which it may be concluded that there were already numerous settlements in the vicinity. However, Moscow itself can hardly have had more than five or six thousand inhabitants.

A century later, Moscow became the capital of a grand principality, one of the most powerful in northeastern Russia, and the center of political and ecclesiastical power.

In this period Russia consisted of eleven grand principalities or duchies, although the development of agriculture, crafts and trade encouraged the trend towards unification.

At this time a new fort, constructed of oak beams, was raised in the center of Moscow, but this lasted less than thirty years. It was destroyed in one of the frequent fires, and in 1367 the new ruler, Dimitrius of the Don (Dmitri Donskoi), ordered the building of white-stone ramparts, hence the name

11. Moscow panorama from the bell-tower of Ivan the Great, in the center of the Kremlin. With its impressive height of 96 m, the Ivanovskaya tower, completed in the reign of Boris Godunov, dominates the whole area.

'Belo-kamen' (white stone) by which Moscow was popularly known at that time. The construction of the new fortifications, which afforded protection against the Mongol-Tartar hordes, attracted thousands of new inhabitants — artisans and merchants. The population of the city rose to between thirty and forty thousand.

From this period, the turn of the fifteenth century, some outstanding cultural monuments have been preserved, such as the Church of the Assumption of the Andronikov Monastery. The golden age of Muscovite architecture and art had begun. The city inspired the celebrated painter Theophanes the Greek: in 1399 he depicted Moscow in frescoes of the Cathedral of the Archangel Michael.

In the fifteenth century Moscow flourished as never before, and after the annexation of Novgorod and Tver, the Muscovite grand prince, Ivan III (1462—1505), assumed the title 'Ruler of All Russia'. His wife was the niece of the last Byzantine emperor, and Moscow soon came to be spoken of as the 'third Rome', which meant that it could be considered a potential capital, both spiritual and temporal, of a universal empire.

Old clock in the Moscow Kremlin.

Like other European countries, Russia drew on the achievements of the Italian Renaissance. Ivan III ('the Great'), an able politician and great patron of the arts, invited Italian architects, craftsmen and engineers to undertake the task of rebuilding the Kremlin. The famous Italian architect, Pietro Antonio Solari, reconstructed the fortress in the best Lombardy style, raising the Nikolskaya and Frolovskaya (later Spasskaya) gate-towers, still admired for their size and harmonious proportions. Italians drew up the plans for and built one of the most famous palaces in the Kremlin, the Granovitaya Palata (Faceted Palace), used today for receptions for the most distinguished foreign guests.

The old Russian masterbuilders, their skill and opinions highly respected by the foreign architects, also had a hand in the Kremlin's reconstruction. It may be noted that it was Russian craftsmen who cast the famous bell for Westminster Abbey in London.

Speaking of cast objects, there are two, remarkable for their dimensions, among the churches and palaces of the Kremlin which were given the epithet 'imperial'. The Emperor Bell, the largest in the world — six meters high and weighing over 200 tons — was cast in the Kremlin between 1733 and 1735. Nearby is the technological wonder of the sixteenth century, the Emperor Cannon, with a caliber of 890 millimeters, which was cast in bronze in 1586. The cannonballs for this piece of heavy artillery each weighed several tons. However, this bell has never been rung, nor was the cannon ever fired.

One of the most beautiful churches in the Kremlin, the Cathedral of the Assumption (Uspenski Sobor), was raised in the Russian national style, adorned with five gilded domes (1475—1479).

The Uspenski Sobor, modeled on the much older cathedral of Vladimir, is where Russian tsars were crowned from the sixteenth century on. Even Peter the Great, who had moved the capital to the completely new city of St Petersburg (Petrograd) in 1712, had his coronation there (1721). The Uspenski Sobor stands in the heart of the Kremlin, on Soborni Square, together with other magnificent churches of the golden age of Muscovite architecture, decorated with frescoes by the most celebrated Russian artists, such as Andrei Rublev, Theophanes the Greek and Prohor of Gorodets.

Above the central cluster of Kremlin buildings rises the octagonal bell-tower of Ivan the Great, erected between 1505 and 1508 by the architect Bono Friazin. The tower was raised to its present height (81 m) at the end of the century at the behest of Tsar Boris Godunov, and served as a watchtower.

The Cathedral of the Archangel Michael (Arkhangelski Sobor) was built in the same period and later, in the seventeenth century, decorated with frescoes by Russian artists. This was the burial place of many tsars — Ivan Kalita, Dmitri Donskoi, Ivan III, Ivan the Terrible and others; 34 tombs of rulers and their families are still preserved here.

Between 1776 and 1787 the great Russian architect M. Kazakov raised the magnificent Senate building, on whose central cupola the Red Flag has flown since the October Revolution. It was here that Lenin had his cabinet.

Not far away is the Great Kremlin Palace, built between 1839 and 1849, its façade, 125 meters long, overlooking the Moskva river. This contains three famous halls — the Georgievskaya, Vladimirskaya and Ekaterinskaya, and formerly provided the magnificent setting for imperial balls. It is now used for receptions for foreign dignitaries.

The only large edifice which stands out by its modern style from the rest of the Kremlin is the Congress Palace, built for the holding of Party

Building the Church of the Resurrection of St John. Miniature from the "Imperial Book", 1528.

Empress (tsarina) with her suite entering church. Scene from an old engraving.

congresses (1959—1961). Its vast hall, seating about 6000, is also used for opera, ballet and concerts.

While the Kremlin churches are characterized by a certain severity of form and a restrained use of color, the nine-domed church on Red Square, outside the fortress walls, is remarkable for its inspired originality and lavish decoration. The Pokrovski Sobor, better known as the Cathedral of St Basil, was raised between 1555 and 1561 by the Russian builders Barma and Postnik. Its domes were painted in the colorful Russian style a century later.

With the completion of the cathedral dedicated to St Basil the Blessed (a 'Holy Fool' whose relics were interred in the vaults), the central Muscovite square was named Krasnaya Ploshchad, which should really be translated Beautiful and not Red Square (the adjective *krasni* means both, but here it did not refer to the color!).

Many legends were later woven around the beauty and fantastic appearance of the Cathedral of St Basil, one of the landmarks of Moscow. According to one of these, Ivan the Terrible, the cathedral's founder, had all the workers blinded so they would never be able to build another such miracle of architecture. This may be true, since the tsar did not earn his epithet 'the Terrible' or 'the Dread' without good reason. In that period it was on the Red Square that verdicts were announced and executions took place — on the spot known as Lobnoye Mesto, the Place of the Skull, very close to St Basil's.

The first books were printed in Russia in the sixteenth century. The priest Ivan Fyodorov and his assistant Peter Mstislavets published *The Apostle*, considered to be the earliest Russian incunabulum, in 1564. The first printing works was also established, but Fyodorov and Mstislavets were soon accused of heresy by the Church and were forced to leave Moscow. The printing house later grew into one of the largest in Europe. In 1687 the Slavonic-Greco-Latin Academy was set up, the first institution of higher education in Russia, and in 1755 the eminent academician Lomonosov founded in Moscow the country's first university.

By the mid-seventeenth century the city had a population of some 200,000. The number of inhabitants grew relatively slowly, the primary reason being the frequent catastrophes, mainly fires and epidemics, such as the devastating plague of 1654.

The growth of Moscow as the political and religious center of Russia was checked during the reign of Peter the Great (1672—1725), who raised a new capital, St Petersburg, in the north, in keeping with his vision of a new Russia open to and linked with the West by sea.

During Peter's minority, while he was still in Moscow, his sister Sophia strove to seize power, and was later banished by Peter for life to the Novodevichi Convent, one of the architectural jewels of the Moscow of that time.

Between 1712 and 1721 the city was the 'second capital'. In contrast to westernized Petrograd, it remained closer to Russian national traditions, a difference that can be felt even today.

Among the 3000 cultural monuments in Moscow is the imposing Triumphal Arch, built between 1827 and 1834 by architect August Bove to commemorate the victory over Napoleon in the war of 1812—1814.

Napoleon entered Moscow in 1812 after the battle of Borodino (c. 100 km from the city), in which both the French and Russian armies suffered enormous losses. Withdrawing from Moscow, the Russian general, Kutuzov, declared: "The loss of Moscow does not mean the loss of Russia, but with the loss of the army — Russia is lost."

Approaching the Kremlin, Bonaparte found an almost deserted city, most of the inhabitants having withdrawn together with the army. Legend has it that the Russians set fire to Moscow as they left it, but historians believe that the conflagration that destroyed two thirds of the city started, as many times before, by accident. The fires raged for six days, consuming almost 10,000 buildings, since almost everything, with the exception of the Kremlin, was made of wood.

Over the next ten years, the face of Moscow changed more rapidly than ever before. Stone and brick buildings replaced the wooden ones, many foundations and public buildings were raised, and new squares and streets were constructed.

The Bolshoi Theater, built by the architect Bove according to the plans of Aleksei Mikhailov, was officially opened in January 1825. During the thirties

Warning gong on a watch-tower.

Entry of Pushkin's birth in the register of the Yelokhov Church of the Annunciation, Moscow.

and forties of the last century, the ballet 'Giselle' and Glinka's operas 'Ivan Susanin' and 'Ruslan and Ludmila' were staged there. In the same period, in addition to the Bolshoi (Great) Theatre, the Little Theatre was built for the performance of plays. Both still attract large number of theatergoers.

Moscow, the home of many famous authors, composers and painters, played a leading role in the shaping of the national culture. Alexander Pushkin, Russia's greatest poet, spent his childhood here and had a deep affection for the city. The nineteenth century was an age of exceptional importance for Moscow, as it was for the whole of Russia. The writers Ostrovski, Saltikov-Shchedrin, Leo Tolstoi, Chekhov and many others lived in the city, and Dostoevski's early years were closely connected with it. Many of these vividly depicted Muscovite life. In his epic novel *War and Peace*, Leo Tolstoi portrayed Moscow in the early nineteenth century and gave a powerfully realistic description of the great fire of 1812: "Moscow, in the month of October, regardless of the fact that there was no government, no church, no wealth, no homes, was the same Moscow it had been in August. Everything was destroyed, except for something that was not material, but powerful and indestructible."

Page from the "Book of Hours", 1565.

Chekhov also lovingly described this city, in which he spent many years. In the short story *Three Years*, he expressed his own feelings when writing about his characters' attachment to Moscow: "They were convinced that Moscow was an exceptional city . . . In the Crimea, in the Caucasus or abroad they were bored, dissatisfied and uncomfortable, and they considered their gray Muscovite climate the pleasantest and most healthy."

The houses of all these writers and the museums and monuments dedicated to them can be found all over Moscow.

The life and work of many great composers centered on Moscow. Glinka, Borodin, Mussorgski, Rimski-Korsakov and Tchaikovski are responsible for the city's worldwide musical reputation. Towards the end of the century, Rachmaninov, Skriabin and others lived and composed here, and Tchaikovski was director of the Moscow Conservatory for a while.

Moscow was likewise the home of many outstanding painters whose works adorn the walls of galleries around the world. The finest collection of these is to be seen in the Tretyakov Gallery, built and donated to Moscow in 1856 by a wealthy art lover, Pavel Tretyakov. Together with his brothers, he dedicated almost forty years to collecting valuable works by national artists.

His brother Sergei (1834—1892) devoted himself to collecting works of art from the West, especially France. These are now kept in the Museum of Fine Arts which bears Pushkin's name. This museum, opened in 1912, today houses over half a million paintings, sculptures and drawings, as well as very valuable numismatic collections from various periods. The many exceptional works in this museum include some from ancient Egypt (3rd—4th c. BC), Renaissance Italian paintings, and canvases by such twentieth-century masters as Chagall, Picasso and Dali.

Moscow today covers an area of some 1000 square kilometers and has almost nine million inhabitants. To use the language of modern urban planning, its lay-out is of the concentric-radial type. Certainly there was no definite plan to start with: houses and streets came into being haphazardly, in response to circumstances and the needs of the population. Roads radiated from the Kremlin, the hub of Moscow, towards various Russian cities, while the concentric circles were formed at first as lines of defense, later becoming Moscow's main streets.

The innermost of these ring roads, circling the very heart of the city, was created by the construction of the Tverski Boulevard in 1796 along the line of a massive stone defensive wall, some 10 kilometers in length, with gates and towers. Today when both gates and towers have long since vanished, only their names survive as a memorial of times past: the Pokrovskaya Gate, Nikitinskaya Doors, etc.

Another ring road called the Sadovoya (Garden), a broad highway along which traffic speeds day and night, runs for 16 kilometers around the central area of Moscow, though it is now difficult to define what the center of the city really is. In the sixteenth century, this too was the line of fortifications, comprising ditches and stockading. When the latter was removed near the beginning of the last century, the ditches were filled in and gardens planted in their stead. Today only the name remains to recall the former gardens, for Moscow has spread not only beyond this ring but outside yet another, known as the Moscow Ring Road, which is all of 200 kilometers in length.

At the start of the present century, Moscow was one of the centers of the revolutionary movement. Its proletariat took an active part in the bourgeois revolution of 1905—1907, which Lenin later called the 'dress rehearsal' for the October Revolution of 1917.

Unlike Petrograd, where the Soviet assumed power with little bloodshed, Moscow was the scene of fierce fighting even after the victory of the October Revolution. The revolutionary forces triumphed here in early November, thanks to the arrival of a detachment of sailors from Petrograd. Half a year later, on February 26, 1918, the Soviet government moved to Moscow from Petrograd, where the situation had become precarious. Thus the Kremlin once more became the seat of political power.

On the Red Square, against the very wall of the Kremlin, stands the mausoleum of Vladimir Ilich Lenin. Designed by architect Aleksei Shusev in the form of a stepped pyramid made of red granite and black Labrador, it assumed its present appearance in 1930, when it replaced the temporary wooden mausoleum raised immediately after Lenin's death on January 21, 1924.

The Moscow Kremlin. Engraving, 17th c.

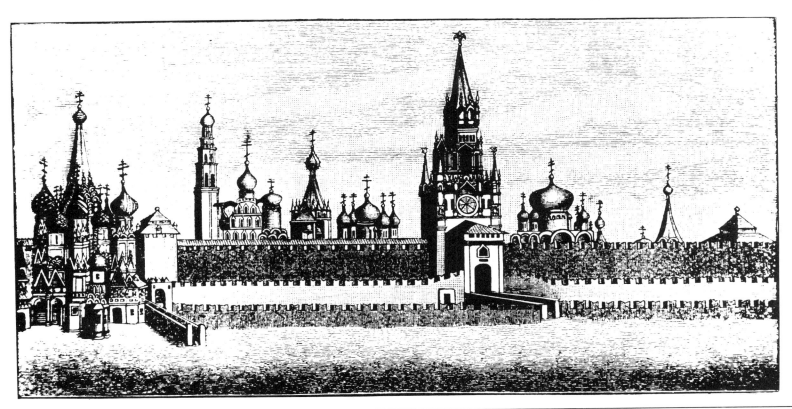

The tomb underwent alterations after the death of Josif Vissarionovich Stalin (1870—1953), when its left side was rearranged in order to receive his sarcophagus. Stalin's remains were removed, however, after the secret report by Nikita Khrushchov to the Congress of the Soviet Communist Party, and were placed in a tomb behind the mausoleum, alongside some other Soviet political figures and generals of World War II.

Most Soviet politicians and eminent persons are interred within the Kremlin walls, where their urns are marked by simple slabs carved with their names. Nikita Khrushchov is the exception, being the only Secretary General buried in the Novodevichi cemetery, where the graves of many distinguished writers, painters, composers, scholars and scientists of the nineteenth and twentieth centuries can be found. A walk through the Novodevichi cemetery is like strolling back through Russian history.

Moscow is today the largest industrial center of the Soviet Union, with many big factories. It is also the country's largest university center: Lomonsov University alone has some 30,000 students. The university building was raised after World War II in neo-classical style on the Lenin Heights. After industry, science is the branch that employs most people in the capital. More than a million Muscovites work in one of the 700 science and research centers, while some 700,000 students attend one of the 75 institutions of higher education in the city.

Over 3000 different magazines, dailies and other periodicals are published in Moscow, in a total of over two billion copies. The trade union paper *Trud* has the largest circulation: 18 million copies daily.

Gilding the roof of the Cathedral of the Assumption, 1551. Miniature from the "Imperial Book".

12.   The Rosija Hotel is among the largest in Moscow, with over 3,000 rooms. A number of small, picturesque churches preserved in the vicinity lend the area a special charm.

13.   The GUM department store, one of the busiest places in Moscow, offers the widest selection of goods to be found in the Soviet Union. Tens of millions of shoppers pass through its arcades every year (pp. 34—35).

14

14. The city streets have not yet been flooded by streams of cars, and the sidewalks are still empty. This Muscovite is making use of the early morning for his favorite 'hobby' — jogging.

15. In Moscow, you can read newspapers in this way, too. Lately, the Soviet press has started to become more open and attracts ever larger numbers of readers.

16. Performances of the Bolshoi Theater are sold out months in advance. Opera and ballet fans are prepared to stand in line for hours in order to obtain tickets, and usually do so in pairs, taking turns in the queue. This student will soon take her friend's place in the line, and in the meantime passes the time by preparing for classes.

15

16

17. A traditional Russian wedding includes many ancient customs. One of the more modern ones, however, is for the bride and groom, after the ceremony, to visit a plateau in the Lenin Hills that offers a magnificent panoramic view of Moscow.

18.   Many young people decide to
embark upon married life in Red
Square, under the walls of the Kremlin.
It has recently also become popular
for them to visit Lenin's mausoleum
and thus pay their respects to the
leader of the October Revolution.

19. The Streets of Moscow are very wide and some even have as many as sixteen lanes. As well as private cars, a large number of trucks drives through the city, increasing the density of the traffic which requires modern and efficient traffic regulation in order to run smoothly.

20.   The Moskva river winds from
northwest to southeast, cutting the city
in two. Muscovites and tourists alike
enjoy trips on 'river trams',
comfortable motor-boats. The Kremlin
and the old part of the city look
particularly attractive from the river.

21

21—22.   The first subway line in Moscow, opened in 1935, was 11 km long and had twelve stations. Today there are ten times as many, and the total length of the underground railway is over 400 km. The Moscow métro transports over six million passengers daily. Many of its stations were designed and decorated by the leading architects and artists of the Soviet Union.

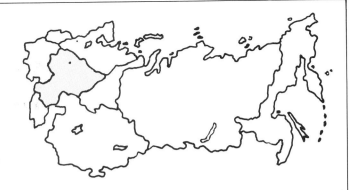

A Journey through History

The Golden Ring

Traveling by horse-drawn coach, it would take seven days to visit the seven historic Russian cities that are the seven jewels in what is called the Golden Ring. These ancient towns and fortresses — Moscow, Zagorsk, Pereslavl Zalesski, Rostov, Yaroslavl, Kostroma and Vladimir — were raised about 70 kilometers apart, the distance that could be covered with good horses in one day.

The road that leads northwest from Moscow to Zagorsk and further is not, in fact, really circular but follows a zigzag route from one to the other of these monuments of early Russian civilization. The epithet 'golden' borne by this remarkable 'ring' alludes not only to the gilded domes and many treasures of these cities but to the role they played in the golden age of a people.

A journey along the Golden Ring is an exciting excursion into the past, an encounter with the national and spiritual centers of ancient Russia.

Today the modern road from Moscow to Zagorsk, 80 kilometers away, can be covered in an hour. Formerly it took a good coachman at least eight hours, and the horses, harnessed to the famous Russian troika, had to be changed half way.

Probably nowhere in the world are there so many songs in praise of coachmen as in Russia, and with good reason. Their vehicles covered the great distances with amazing speed, even by modern standards, as illustrated by the following event.

Towards the end of the sixteenth century, the first emissaries of the English queen passed along the Archangel road. In keeping with the rules of hospitality, Tsar Ivan Vassilevich ordered that the 'English foreigners' were to be assisted on their journey from the port on the White Sea to Moscow. Thanks to the troika, they covered this enormous distance in just a few days. Later the English envoy informed his queen that "the well-organized coach service in Russia ensures a speed with which the countries of Europe cannot compete". No wonder he was impressed: the Englishmen covered over 200 kilometers a day on the snow-bound roads.

The Russian troika is a symbol of old Russia. One of the most famous poetic metaphors of 'Holy Russia' is Gogol's comparison of his homeland with a racing troika that roams the steppes, urged on by the crack of the driver's whip, accompanied by the somewhat melancholy jingle of the horses' bells.

The first sight of Zagorsk (formerly Radonezh) is always a thrilling surprise. Until recently the seat of the Patriarchate of the Russian Orthodox Church (now moved to the Danilovski Monastery in Moscow), this old town, remarkable for its beauty, harmonious contours and multi-colored domes, comes suddenly into view under the wide sky.

Six hundred years ago, the monk Sergei of Radonezh founded here the

23. Muscovites are great lovers of the seventh art. In recent years, the Moscow International Film Festival has gained increasingly high prestige worldwide.

Monastery of the Trinity (Troitsko-Sergyevskaya Lavra). The oldest of the monastery's churches, the Cathedral of the Holy Trinity, was built on the same site in 1422, the year when Sergei of Radonezh was canonized and officially proclaimed the Protector of Russian Lands. For the cathedral's iconostasis, the greatest medieval Russian artist, Andrei Rublev, painted his famous Old Testament Holy Trinity, often interpreted as expressing his enduring belief in the harmony of the World and the indestructibility of Beauty. Today the original is to be seen in the Tretyakov Gallery in Moscow; the Holy Trinity on the iconostasis is an exact copy.

The six hundredth anniversary of Andrei Rublev, the most celebrated Russian icon-painter, was commemorated in Moscow in September 1960, although the exact date of his birth is not known, only the date on which he died (January 29, 1430) and the place where he was buried — the Spaso-Andronikov Monastery in Moscow, which now houses a gallery of his works.

"Khazan Cat", lubok (wood-cut) 18th c.

Rublev's name is wreathed in legend. Already in the fifteenth century his paintings were literally worth their weight in gold. So great were his fame and reputation that when the question of how the Trinity should be depicted was debated by the Church Synod in Moscow in 1551, it was ruled that painters should emulate the traditional models of the Greek (i. e. Byzantine) artists and the work of Andrei Rublev.

Of all Rublev's opus, the Old Testament Trinity is certainly the best known, most valuable, and most frequently taken as epitomizing the whole of old Russian painting. The exact year when it was completed is unknown. Some scholars date it towards the end of the fourteenth century, although several written sources place it at the beginning of the fifteenth. In any case, the icon stood for more than five hundred years in the Holy Trinity-Sergiev Monastery, until it was transferred to Moscow in 1929. It has been restored several times; its present form, according to experts, is close but not identical to that created by the great artist.

Sergiev Pasad, as Zagorsk was called until the Revolution, originated, like most other towns of that age, as a stronghold against foreign invaders. Surrounded by massive walls, in places twelve meters high, this fortress managed to withstand a sixteen-month Polish siege (1608—1610), during which time the Russian people looked to the Trinity-Sergiev Monastery as a symbol of national independence. An obelisque in the center of Zagorsk commemorates those troubled times.

"A Bear and Goat Enjoying Themselves", Russian lubok, first half of the 18th c.

Thanks to the privileges and endowments it was granted by the tsars, the monastery gradually became a powerful feudal landowner, and in the sixteenth and seventeenth centuries also a flourishing center of icon-painting, manuscript copying and the production of ornamental wooden artifacts. Apart from Rublev, another great icon-painter, Daniel Chorni, who with his pupils decorated many Russian churches, was invited to work here.

Other ancient monuments in this extraordinarily harmonious architectural ensemble are the Cathedral of the Holy Ghost, raised by builders from Pskov (1476—1477), and the five-domed Cathedral of the Assumption, begun in the reign of Ivan the Terrible (1559) and completed a quarter of a century later. Close by is the burial vault of the Godunovs — Tsar Boris, his wife Xenia and their children. Neither Boris nor members of his family were popular among the people. The tragedy of this ruler was later immortalized in literature by the greatest Russian poet, Alexander Pushkin. However, the name of the tsarina, Xenia Borisovna, a woman of exceptional beauty and skilled in embroidery, has been remembered with more favor. An altar cloth worked by her, today displayed in the Zagorsk museum, is exquisitely embroidered in silk, gold and silver thread on black velvet, and encrusted with jewels.

One of the oldest public buildings in the monastery complex is the hospital with the Chapel of SS Zosimus and Savatius (1635—1637). From the same period date the Church of St John the Forerunner (Baptist) above the entrance to the monastery, and the palace of Tsar Aleksei Mikhailovich, who used to stay there with a suite of five hundred people. Not far away is the palace of the Metropolitan, an original structure that took over three hundred years to complete: the ground floor dates from the sixteenth century, the first from the seventeenth, and the second from the eighteenth.

Also worthy of note are the tiny Church of St Micah, which seems to have been raised as a contrast to the sumptuous Refectory, and the Church of the Virgin of Smolensk.

No great distance from the Golden Ring lie Pushkino, Bratovshchina, Rachmanovo, Muranovo, Gzhel, Abramtsovo ... This last place, only 15 kilometers from Zagorsk, was once the estate of the celebrated Aksakov family.

The little place of Gzhel near Moscow has been renowned for centuries for its majolica, considered among the finest achievements of folk arts and crafts. This pottery — figures from village life and mythology — has preserved its traditions and high quality thanks to the craftsmen: they have never made two identical figures. Gzhel semi-faience is particularly valuable but can mostly be found only in the museums of the Golden Ring towns, although this traditional craft, like others, has been gradually revived in recent years.

* * *

Pereslavl Zalesski, the second in the row of jewels of the Golden Ring, is one of the most ancient towns in Russia: according to chronicles it was founded in 1152.

The oldest cultural monument here is the Cathedral of the Transfiguration, raised in the center of the town in 1152—1157 by an almost dry-stone technique. The blocks of white limestone were placed one on top of another and the cracks between them filled in with chippings and then coated with an original adhesive mixture.

Not far from this cathedral, which served as the model for old Russian architecture in the northeast, stands the monument to Alexander Nevski, the legendary military commander, celebrated even in his lifetime by historians and popular story-tellers alike. Grand Prince Alexander of Vladimir (1220—1263), who led the Russian army against the Swedes and Teutonic Knights, gained the name Nevski from his victory in a crucial battle on the Neva river in 1240. He is one of the few military commanders canonized by the Russian Orthodox Church. In his *Life*, written toward the end of the thirteenth century, he was presented as the ideal prince and military leader, the Protector of Russian Lands. Shortly before World War II, the famous film director Sergei Eisenstein made a movie about Alexander Nevski, who was born in Pereslavl, and in 1942 the Soviet government introduced a military decoration bearing the name of this medieval prince.

The sixteenth century also left its mark on the architecture of Pereslavl. On the orders of Ivan the Terrible, the beautiful buildings and mighty walls of the Monastery of St Nikita, originally founded in the twelfth century, were raised just north of the town. The monastery, to which the tsar gave land, villages and craftsmen, became one of the main feudal strongholds in the 1560s.

Smolensk, from an old engraving.

Pereslavl Zalesski gave Russia many famous craftsmen, especially masons, and also experienced sailors who fished in nearby Lake Pleshcheyevo in the large wooden boats they built themselves. When the young Peter I decided in the late seventeenth century that Russia must have a strong fleet, he found good shipbuilders in Pereslavl. Before setting off north, to the estuary of the Neva, Peter first constructed a miniature fleet on this lake. The Little Ships of Peter I Museum is a reminder of this event, while nearby, on Mount Gremyach, the model vessel 'Fortuna' dropped anchor for the last time. Among the museum's exhibits are the tools which belonged to the young tsar and some of the fine wooden carvings that ornamented his ships.

* * *

Only two cities of ancient Russia are called Great: one is Novgorod, the other Rostov, which *The Tale of Bygone Times* mentions, along with Kiev, as early as 862.

The importance of Rostov the Great in the formation of the old Russian state can be seen from the fact that in the mid-tenth century Constantinople

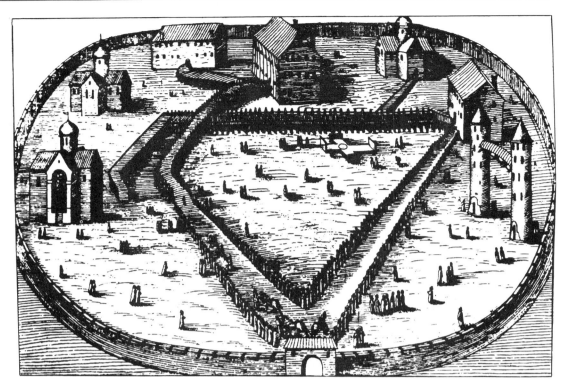

Alexandrovsk settlement, engraving from 1627.

was obliged to pay tribute to this town on the shore of Lake Nero, far from the Black Sea. This followed Prince Oleg's campaign in which the capital of the great Byzantine Empire was captured and Oleg's shield placed on the gates of the city.

The first independent Rostov prince was Yuri Dolgoruki, during whose reign the town gained the attribute Great. But Yuri, not trusting the Rostov boyars (feudal-court nobility), chose Suzdal as his seat, so that the principality was known as Rostov-Suzdal. Popular tradition gives Rostov the principal role in defending the land in this period (mid-12th c.). The heroes of folk songs, Iliya Muromets and Alyosha Popovich, came from Rostov the Great.

Some exceptional Rostov women have also entered Russian history. The Princesses Darya Rostovska and Antonina Puzhbolska, dressed as men, fought bravely at the battle of Kulikovo in 1380. In the seventeenth century, Irina Lugovska repeated their feat: in male attire she took part in the battle for Smolensk. Widowed young, Irina Lugovska dedicated her life to raising churches in Rostov, and gave the master-builders a Dutch Piscator Bible. The illustrations in this Bible had a great influence on later fresco-painting in Rostov churches.

The Rostov Kremlin stands out among the masterpieces of Russian architecture by its rare and highly original domes of gold and silver, edged with elaborate crosses.

Rostov is likewise famed for its bell-towers and the traditional art of bell-ringing. Even Peter I, who after a defeat ordered all the bells in Russia to be melted down to make arms, did not have the heart to include those of Rostov. Great Russian composers — Glinka, Mussorgski, Rachmaninov — were inspired by the chimes of the 'singing metal' and used these in their works. Musicians from the West came to Rostov the Great to hear the unique concert of its bells. The art of bell-ringing was passed down from generation to generation. In the second half of the nineteenth century, special glockenspiels were constructed in Rostov, perfectly imitating the church bells of this city. These unusual musical instruments, which won prizes at the World Exhibitions in Vienna (1873) and Philadelphia (1876), are kept today in the local museum.

Rostov the Great is also noted for a traditional art that has been preserved here — finifti, decorative and portrait painting in enamel. In olden times, weapons, religious objects, church vessels, covers of valuable books, medallions and jewelry were all decorated in this manner. Today the tradition is carried on by the master-craftsmen of the Rostov enamel factory.

* * *

The coat-of-arms of Kostroma is painted on a blue shield, with a gilded wooden ship cutting the silver waves, an eagle's head on the prow and seven rowers below the sail. Kostroma used to be called the 'Linen Capital of the North' because of the high-quality linen sails it exported to the West. The English, renowned sailors, once sent a barrel of gold in exchange for these sails. It was their gift to the hard-working sailmakers, who used this gold to build the Church of the Resurrection in 1692.

Kostroma and the surrounding villages were also noted for their goldsmiths, known far and wide for their gold and silver jewelry and ornaments. The village of Krasnoye on the Volga was the center of this craft. As early as the seventeenth century, the workshops of this area were producing gold wine-goblets, silver wine-jugs, colorful bowls with folk motifs, ornamental boxes with fairy-tale figures, and other articles. Almost every village household had its cottage industry: in one, they worked silver, in another they did wood-carving, in a third, basket-weaving . . . Today this village has a unique school for the artistic craft of metalworking.

* * *

Suzdal is often described as a museum-town because of its many cultural monuments dating from the twelfth to nineteenth centuries. For all who travel along the Golden Ring it is certainly a place not to be missed. The history of the town, placed under state protection because of its cultural value, is similar to that of the other ancient Russian cities, of which Suzdal is among the oldest, being mentioned in chronicles as early as 1024. For a time the religious capital of medieval Russia, Suzdal with its innumerable churches and monasteries is a vivid reminder of bygone times, of great princes and dukes, and above all of the builders who raised it. The harmonious beauty of these buildings is still quite unspoilt.

Monastic scribe. Drawing from the 14th c.

In the area of Suzdal there are several dozen important architectural works that reflect the past life and history of the town. Many of the churches are decorated with frescoes, the earliest dating from the thirteenth century. Some of the Suzdal churches, such as St Nicholas in the village of Glotovo, are built entirely of wood in the traditional manner, without the use of a single nail. The Convent of the Intercession (Pokrovski Monastir) on the bank of the river Kamenka is outstanding, even here, for its beauty. Founded in 1364 and enlarged over the centuries to form a perfect architectural whole, it resembles a lavish theatrical set of almost unreal beauty. Many famous women took refuge or were confined in the Convent of the Intercession, which is the burial place of Ivan the Terrible's first wife, Boris Godunov's daughter, and the wife of Tsar Basil (Vasili) Shuski. It was here that the first wife of Peter the Great, Evdokia Lopukhina, was confined until she was eventually rescued by her grandson, Peter II, and spent the rest of her life in Moscow, in the Novodevichi Convent.

* * *

The town of Yaroslavl is also almost one thousand years old, having been founded in 1010 by Yaroslav the Wise, but its period of blossoming came six centuries later, with the completion of the architectural ensemble which turned this city on the Volga into one of the loveliest in old Russia.

The monastery archives preserve the most valuable work of early Russian literature, *The Lay of Igor's Campaign*, an epic describing Prince Igor's campaign against the Polovtsi in 1185. The author is unknown, but is thought to have been someone from the suite of Prince Svyatoslav of Kiev. Written in rhythmic prose, this richly metaphorical work stresses the need for the Russian principalities to unite. The original manuscript, discovered in 1795, was destroyed in the Moscow fire of 1812.

* * *

In the early twelfth century a new center of the future Great Russia began to rise in the northeast. This was Vladimir, a town that rivaled Kiev in the strength of its fortifications and beauty and number of its churches. In 1160, Prince Andrei Bogolyubski brought together 'master-craftsmen from all lands' to build the three-domed Cathedral of the Assumption, its façades and interior richly ornamented with stone figures and reliefs, frescoes and gold.

Initial from a 12th-century manuscript.

Three hundred years later, the Italian architect Aristotel Fioravanti from Bologna was to sketch the most important features and details of the church and incorporate them in his own Cathedral of the Assumption in the Moscow Kremlin.

The Virgin of Vladimir, the work of an unknown Byzantine icon-painter from the early twelfth century, was long kept in the Cathedral of the Assumption (Uspenski Sobor) in the city of Vladimir (named after its founder, Prince Vladimir Monomakh), and is now in Moscow's Tretyakov Gallery. This cathedral, which was intended to surpass the Kievan Cathedral of St Sophia in beauty and size, is one of the most magnificent buildings of old Russia. A chronicler declared that "there is none such in Russia, and never will be". In the early fifteenth century, Andrei Rublev and Daniel Chorni were invited to decorate this cathedral; their stay resulted in some exceptional frescoes, unfortunately only partly preserved. The central part contains a fresco of the Last Judgement, a work outstanding for its composition, execution and coloring, despite damage and the passage of time. An icon of the Virgin and Child by Andrei Rublev is also preserved here.

Not far from the Uspenski Sobor is another exceptional cultural monument of old Vladimir, the Cathedral of St Dmitri, built (1194—1197) by Prince Vsevolod as a royal chapel, and intended to demonstrate the power and wealth of the Grand Prince of Vladimir. It is therefore exceptionally richly decorated, with over 1300 reliefs, including some complex compositions, such as the myth of the ascent of Alexander of Macedonia to heaven.

The Monastery of the Nativity was also built in the twelfth century, and until the fourteenth was the seat of the Patriarch of the Russian Church. A chronicle of those time was written in this monastery, and in November 1263 the body of Alexander Nevski was laid to rest here. His remains were later moved to St Petersburg.

The village of Paleh has been called the 'golden nest' of Russian folk art. From here fabulous firebirds, figurines from fairy-tale and legend, tsars and heroes make their way to other parts of the country. Paleh is a village of self-taught artists — naive painters, although there are some members of the Artists' Association among them. In a way, the art of painting on boxes, decorative panels and jewelry is a continuation of the art of icon-painting.

The artistic procedure of the Paleh masters requires careful and lengthy preparation, which is completed by covering the boxes with black lacquer. Then natural pigments mixed with egg-yolk are used for the precise, detailed outlines, which are later filled in with vivid colors. The subjects are mostly Russian folk tales, traditional genre scenes and, in more recent times, contemporary subjects as well. Certain miniatures, figures and inscriptions can be clearly seen only with the aid of a magnifying glass. Each of these highly valued handcraft products is signed by the artist, with a note that it was made in Paleh.

Paleh art was born in the late eighteenth century with the manufacture of lacquered snuff-boxes. In the villages of Paleh, Mstyora and Holuy, this craft has been preserved to the present day, and in the last fifty years has developed into a real art form which has received recognition in Paris, Venice, New York and other cities. Of the 20,000 articles produced in Paleh, more than a quarter are sold to western countries.

24. One of the symbols of Russia is the river Volga. It rises somewhere in the vast forests of the north, makes a quiet and dignified progress through the Russian plains, and after many thousands of kilometers, flows into the Caspian Sea.

25. Sky, earth and water create a uniquely harmonious beauty in the surroundings of the ancient city of Vladimir. The lovely Moscow region has always inspired Russian poets and artists, among them Puskhin and Repin. The population were traditionally farmers, artisans and fishermen, and many old customs and crafts have been preserved to this day (pp. 54—55).

26. The people of 'Greater Russia', the teritory of the former Muscovite principality, led hard lives for centuries. Of all European lands, Russia was the last to abolish the feudal ties of the peasant to the landowner's estate. Patriarchal values were long present in the consciousness of the Russian peasant (pp. 56—57).

Medieval Russian warriors used spears to fight invaders. Swedes, Germans and Danes attacked from the north, the Mongol hordes from the east.

27—28. *The Volga watershed abounds in rivers and streams. In the fall, the rising waters flood the fertile plain, preparing it for a new cycle of growth. The Russians often refer to the Volga as 'matushka', meaning 'little mother', as it has always proved bountiful to those who sought a living on its banks. The churches in this watershed bear witness to the spiritual development of the people living along the river.*

29. *The Russian winter is long and severe, but the frost brings some compensation along with the hardships: playing its tricks with the waters and nature, it offers us an incomparable vision of the world around us (pp. 60—61).*

30

30. In the sixteenth century, Emperor Ivan the Terrible had a summer residence built for himself in the village of Kolomenskoye, south of Moscow. The striking Church of the Ascension was also raised, in 1533. The wooden summer house has vanished, but the Kolomenskoye church still withstands the passage of time.

31. The birch, that ubiquitous feature of Russian art, has been one of the most highly valued trees since olden times. The trunks were used for building houses and bridges, the bark for making 'lapti', a kind of traditional peasant shoe, and the roots for balms . . .

32. Horses, the eternal symbol of freedom and wide-open spaces, often figure in Russian tales and legends. This scene is from a film by the famous Soviet director, Andrei Tarkovski (pp. 64—65).

34

33. Windmills are not found only in Holland, nor were they attacked by Spaniards alone. This old wooden mill near Kostroma, still in use, is powered by the strong westerly winds which, according to legend, are sent by the god Perun.

34—35. Summer in 'Greater Russia' is a time of golden wheat, luxuriant vegetation and colorful wild flowers. Thanks to the continental climate, the summers are hot and dry, but the rivers provide enough moisture for the fertile land.

33

35

36

36. The troika symbolizes the vast
expanses of the Russian lowlands. The
great writer Nikolai Gogol compared it
with Russia itself: under the crack of
the driver's whip, it roams the
wide-open spaces to the melancholy
jingling of tiny bells.

37. Old Suzdal is one of the brightest
jewels in the 'Golden Ring'
surrounding Moscow: its first churches
were raised almost a thousand years
ago. Prince Yuri Dolgoruki made it the
capital of his principality,
Rostov-Suzdal, which was later to grow
into an empire.

38

38—39. Seals are not confined to polar regions — they can also be seen in frozen inlets of the Caspian Sea. This type of seal has lived along the shores of the largest 'inland' sea since times immemorial.

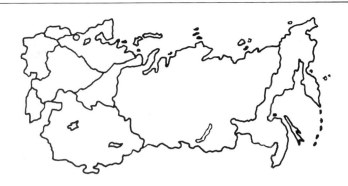

The City of White Nights
Leningrad

"On the bank of the Neva, before the fortress built by Peter Alexeyevich, in the midst of the city which on his orders two hundred thousand Russian peasants were forced to raise at the cost of gruesome sacrifices, rises an immense granite rock from which the creator of the Empire readies himself for a tremendous leap; high rears the steed, firmly checked by the hand of its master; a powerful will bends the beast into submission; each muscle of the bodies of horse and rider is strained to the utmost; invincible seems this gigantic figure, whose knees let the horse know that it must not resist its master's will. Wide swings the imperious right hand of the emperor. Nothing, it seems, can stop this rider from destroying any enemy who should oppose him. This is the moment of unrestrained and inexhaustible power, an unbreakable will of iron. The rider on the granite rock comes from a vast land ruled by his will — stretching as far as the shores of the Black Sea, to the borders of Persia and China, across the Urals to the very depths of Siberia. It has been forgotten that his man, at the end of his life, screaming with pain, died in agony of cancer of the bladder, forgotten how millions cursed this man, in whom they saw an emissary of Hell, the Antichrist, shuddering with fear and loathing at the very thought of him."

With these words the German writer Kurt Kerstner begins his historical study of Peter the Great, one of Russia's most important rulers, a man who profoundly influenced not only the development of his country but also its position in Europe. The city on the Neva, first named St Petersburg, began to take shape in 1703. Never before had a city been created under such careful supervision by its founder. Never, in all probability, did the destiny of a great city depend to such an extent on the wishes, vision and ideas of one man.

Peter I, a member of the Romanov family, was born in 1672 and died in 1725. He ascended the throne at the age of seventeen after staging a coup against his elder sister, Sophia (1689). In tribute to his great social and economic reforms, Peter is always called the Great, an epithet appropriate to his stature of two meters as well as to his achievements for his country. More than any ruler before him, he saw Russia's future in closer ties with the West, in the adoption of its advances in technology and production, in the education of his own people, and in reforms which wrought fundamental changes in the thousand-year-old fabric of patriarchal and feudal life. Peter himself often set an example as to how progressive ideas of the age should be studied and put into practice. Though he frequently resorted to cruel and despotic methods to attain his ends, such was the time in which he lived.

Peter I's reforms marked a crucial phase in Russia's development, bringing far-reaching changes to the lives of its sixteen million inhabitants (1725). A roll was made of all serfs, taxes were introduced, and the peasantry was compelled to pay for the equipment of recruits in the standing army as

40. From its foundation in 863, Smolensk became the Russian 'stone shield' towards the west. The history of the town is a chronicle of wars against numerous conquerors; many battles decisive for the fate of Russia were fought under its walls.

well as to work, in shifts, building St Petersburg and other towns. An imperial decree of 1714 made the estates of the court nobility hereditary, but stipulated that they could not be broken up. This meant that many noblemen were obliged to acquire an education and engage in some profession.

In 1722 Peter introduced the 'table of ranks' regulating government service, which divided all who served the state into fourteen groups and allowed gradual promotion from lower to higher ranks. Analogous ranks were introduced in the army as well. Since rich peasants and merchants became hereditary noblemen on reaching the eighth rank, this encouraged a degree

The Nevski Prospekt, Anichkov Palace. Engraving after a drawing by M. I. Makhaev, mid-18th c.

of social mobility. Peter I demanded that his courtiers should acquire a certain amount of education, and those who avoided studying or failed to 'master numbers and some parts of geometry' were even forbidden to marry.

In twenty-five years of his reign, more than 100 manufacturing plants were opened, some with as many as 10,000 workers (the Admiralty Shipyard). Iron smelting reached an output of almost 13,000 tons, and by the mid-eighteenth century Russia was producing two million tons of pig iron a year, exporting some of it to Great Britain.

In Peter's reign Russia warred on both its northern and southern borders, fighting the Swedes, the Prussians, the Turks ... It was in his time that the Russians started moving towards the East and Central Asia, and broadened their trade links with China and India. The country was expanding.

The founding of St Petersburg, the 'Window on the West' represented the successful conclusion of Russia's centuries-long struggle for an outlet on the Baltic, an ambition dictated by both economic and political interests. Between 1712 and 1728, and later, from 1732 to 1918, St Petersburg was the capital of the Russian state.

This city, frequently called the 'Venice of the North', lies on forty-two islands crisscrossed by almost a hundred canals. With over five million inhabitants, it is the second largest city in the Soviet Union, after Moscow. Following the death of the leader of the October Revolution, it was renamed Leningrad.

The city on the Neva was created as the first industrial town of Russia. Brickworks, shipyards and military establishments were the first to be raised. By the end of the eighteenth century there were over 160 enterprises, which operated on the basis of serf labor. The population grew from 40,000 in 1725 to 220,000 in 1800. When Peter made St Petersburg the new capital, the imperial court, ministries, Senate and other government institutions were all transferred from Moscow. Later the Winter and Summer Palaces, the Hermitage, and numerous other splendid edifices were built, many of which still grace the city.

View of the Great Palace from the Gulf of Finland. Engraving after a drawing by M. I. Makhaev.

Soon after the founding of St Petersburg, a number of educational institutions were established to train specialists in various fields: the Naval Academy (1715), School of Engineering (1719), Artillery School (1721) and others. The year 1725 saw the opening of the Academy of Science. Today, 2800 doctors of science and over 20,000 masters of science work in the scientific institutions of Leningrad and its economy.

In the eighteenth and, especially, the nineteenth centuries, St Petersburg was the center of Russian culture, particularly literature. The Petrograd writers of this age left an indelible imprint on nineteenth-century literature, not only in Russia but worldwide. It is enough to mention Pushkin, Gogol, Lermontov, Turgenev, Dostoevski ...

The first permanent theater in Russia opened its doors in St Petersburg in 1756, followed a year later by the first Art Academy, where great names of Russian realist painting received their training.

The first Russian museum was also founded in this city, which now has some fifty permanent museums, and in 1814 the first public library was opened. A hundred years earlier, the first hospitals had been established here. As all this shows, the city on the Neva led the way in many fields of life at the beginning of the modern age in Russia.

Leningrad is certainly one of the loveliest cities in the Soviet Union. Its magnificent buildings, spacious squares, parks, rivers and canals, bridges, exquisite wrought-iron railings, statues, monuments, churches — all these give it the unique, unforgettable beauty for which it is famed far beyond the borders of its own country.

The Hermitage — is one of the world's richest museums of the fine arts, housing over two and a half million exhibits from many different countries and periods. The history of the Hermitage starts with the building of the Winter Palace, designed by architect Bartolomeo Rastrelli (1700—1771) in exuberant Baroque style. An imperial residence from 1762 until the October Revolution, it was extended and reconstructed on several occasions. What is today called the Hermitage encompasses three other buildings apart from this palace — the Little, Old and New Hermitages. All these are interconnected to form the unique complex of the richest and largest museum in the USSR.

The origin of the Hermitage collection dates back to 1764, when a Berlin merchant bought 225 works of art for Empress Catherine II. Somewhat later, several art collections were purchased on behalf of the empress in England,

France and other countries. All this was considered her private property and was far removed from the eyes of the public. "Only myself and the mice admire all this," Catherine once wrote.

With the growth of her collection, kept in her private residence, the Little Hermitage, more space was needed, and the Old Hermitage building was raised. The collection was further enlarged in the late eighteenth century by the acquisition of works of art from Greece and Scythian culture. Particularly important is the collection of Scythian gold, found in ancient towns near the northern shores of the Black Sea. Around this time the Hermitage collection was enriched with art objects from Egypt and Mesopotamia, Byzantium, Syria and other oriental lands. After the entry of the Russian army into Paris and Napoleon's defeat in 1814, the Hermitage acquired a number of works from the Paris collection of Empress Josephine. In the following decades, works of

The equestrian statue of Peter the Great, the founder of St Petersburg, unveiled in 1782. It inspired the poet Alexander Pushkin to write a poem about this great personnage.

The building of the Schliselburg lock at St Petersburg, early 19th c.

art were purchased in Spain and Italy, among them several by Leonardo (the Madonna Litta) and Raphael (the Madonna Conestabile).

After the October Revolution of 1917, the Hermitage also acquired a great number of valuable works from private collections. During the Second World War and the siege of Leningrad, 1.118,000 works of art were evacuated to the Urals for safekeeping.

The Hermitage today houses 15,000 paintings, 12,000 sculptures, 600,000 sketches and drawings, over 600,000 archeological finds, about one million different coins and medals, and over 224,000 objects of applied art.

The part of the museum exhibiting Russian works of art from the sixth century to the present day is particularly rich. A great number of icons, old jewelry, weapons, maps and medical instruments are displayed here. Separate sections are devoted to Peter the Great, Mikhail Lomonosov, and other eminent figures of Russian history and civilization.

The Hermitage also contains numerous objects belonging to prehistoric cultures, the art and civilization of the peoples of Central Asia (4000 BC to the early 20th c.), the Golden Hordes (13th—14th c.), the Caucasian peoples (1100 BC to the 19th c.), Egypt (4000 BC to the 4th c. AD), China (2000 BC to the 20th c.), Mongolia, Japan and Indonesia (800—200 BC), Rome (700 BC to the 4th c. AD), etc.

The treasures of Western European art and culture from the eleventh to the twentieth century include paintings by Leonardo da Vinci, Raphael, Titian, Caravaggio, Michaelangelo, Giogione, Veronese, El Greco, Goya, Velasquez, Murillo, Rembrandt, Rubens, Van Eyk, Delacroix, Renoir, Degas, Monet, Manet, Gauguin, Matisse, Picasso, Chagall and many others.

The city of St Petersburg — Leningrad is an open-air museum in itself. The Winter Palace and Admiralty, the Kazan Cathedral and Mikhailov Castle, the buildings surrounding the Square of the Arts — Dekabrists, where Fyodor Dostoevski awaited execution until his last-minute reprieve came through and he was sent to Siberia instead, the Street of the Builders of Russia and Palace Square — all these are true artistic creations. Bronze monuments on the squares, marble statues in the Summer Garden, the lacelike iron railings of old buildings, the lamps in the steets and on the bridges, the parks and the fountains — all this makes up the great city which has also been called the 'Versailles of the North'.

The Peterhof Palace lies 29 kilometers from Leningrad, on the shore of the Gulf of Finland. Its construction started in 1709 on the orders of Peter I, who wanted to have a summer residence like those of European monarchs — Versailles, for example. Many famous builders from Russia and the West were engaged, and the work was carried out under the tsar's personal supervision. Constructed on an elevation above the sea, the Grand Palace, the central building of this splendid architectural ensemble, was extended and reconstructed on several occasions. The celebrated architect Rastrelli gave the building its Russian Baroque appearance (1747—1752). But Peter seems to have preferred and spent more time in a much more modest building than this summer palace: the Monplaisir rest-house, also constructed in his reign.

Peterhof's dazzling beauty is enhanced by its many fountains (over 170), the water supply having been ensured by the digging of a 22-kilometer canal (1721). From the palace down to the shore tumbles the Grand Cascade, decorated with fountains, gilded statues and bas-reliefs (Rastrelli). The cascades flow into a pool, in the center of which stands the monumental sculpture

Works on the Fontanka river near the Anichkov Palace. Engraving after a drawing by M. I. Makhaev, mid-18th c.

'Samson Tearing Apart the Lion's Jaws', an allegory of the victory over the Swedes in the battle of Poltava (1710).

The construction of the Peter-Paul Fortress began on May 10, 1703, the date which is taken to mark the foundation of Petrograd. In later times the fortress was mostly used as a jail for political prisoners. In the Cathedral of SS Peter and Paul within its walls, all the rulers from Peter I to Alexander III were buried.

Pushkin, Pavlovsk, Razliv, Repino — these are only a few of the places around Leningrad which have shared the eventful history of the city on the Neva. Pushkin, the former Tsarskoye Selo (Imperial Village), was raised at the same time as St Petersburg. In 1811 the Imperial Lycée was opened here, in which Alexander Pushkin studied for six years. From 1834 to 1837 another great Russian poet, Lermontov, lived here. Around this time Tsarskoye Selo was connected to Petrograd by the first railway in Russia.

The city was the center of the October Revolution which in 1917 'shook the world', as US journalist John Reed says in his book.

Although Russia entered the capitalist system very late, towards the end of the nineteenth century, it soon became one of the strongest imperialist countries. Big capital and large numbers of workers were concentrated in Petrograd and Moscow. Under such conditions, the call of the Bolsheviks for peace and social justice was welcomed by most of the population.

After the 'February Revolution' in March 1917 (Russia was at that time still using the old calendar, which was two weeks behind the new), Tsar Nicholas II was forced to abdicate, and later placed under arrest, and a provisional government headed by Kerenski was formed.

On the night of November 6/7 (old style October 25/26), to the thunder of cannon from the cruiser 'Avrora', the workers stormed the Winter Palace in Petrograd. Just a few hours later, at Smolni, the congress of the soviet of military, workers' and peasants' deputies issued three historic decrees: on peace, land reform, and the formation of the Soviet Government.

Only twenty-five years later, Leningrad endured probably the most terrible period in its history. During the nine-hundred-day siege of the city (1941—1943), almost a million of its inhabitants died of starvation, disease or fighting Hitler's forces. The Piskaryevsko cemetery with its mass graves of Leningrad's war victims is a moving reminder of this tragic event.

Leningrad itself did not suffer very extensive damage during the Second World War, but the outlying areas were devastated at the time of the German blockade of the city. The palaces and parks of Pushkin (the former Tsarskoye Selo), Peterhof, Gatchina, Pavlovsk — ensembles that have been compared with Versailles — were reduced to ruins. After the war, it was not a matter of repairing the damage but of completely rebuilding them. On the basis of old plans, drawings, engravings and photographs, all these architectural gems were recreated down to the last detail.

41. *Leningrad, formerly St Petersburg or Petrograd, was the first truly European city on Russian soil. The elite of artists and poets made their homes here, among them Alexander Pushkin, as the inhabitants proudly point out. Many even refer to the town as 'Pushkin's City'.*

АЛЕКСАНДРУ СЕРГѢЕВИЧУ

ПУШКИНУ.

Младыхъ бесѣдъ оставя блескъ и шумъ
Я зналъ и трудъ, и вдохновенье
И сладостно мнѣ было жаркихъ думъ
Уединенное волненье.

43

42—43. Leningrad, said to be one of the most beautiful cities in the world, is famed for its unique architectural harmony, its wide avenues, riverside embankments, and many bridges. The Cathedral of St Isaac, one of the jewels of the city, is among the largest churches in Europe. Its architects, O. Monferrant and V. Spasov, spent thirty-eight years on its construction. Consecrated in 1858, St Isaac's is the last building of Russian Classicism.

44—45.   The Summer Garden in the heart of the city is a rare example of the type of park laid out in the late eighteenth century. Dozens of marble statues by noted sculptors, the richly ornamented wrought-iron railings surrounding it, and its shady avenues, all add to its attraction. The Summer Garden is mentioned in Pushkin's 'Eugene Onegin' and 'Queen of Spades' as a place of romantic assignations and fashionable leisure.

46

46. The Bronze Horseman was raised in 1782 in honor of the great reformer of Russia, Emperor Peter the Great. This imposing equestrian statue was the work of the eminent sculptors Falconet and M. Kollo.

47. Detail of one of the two lighthouses on Vasilyevski Island. These lighthouses no longer serve as such, but are preserved as historical monuments of the city.

48. The promenades along the river Neva are embellished by richly ornamented wrought-iron railings. The most beautiful and best known among them seem to compete in the originality and inventiveness of their iron ornamentation.

17

18

49

49—50. The Hermitage, one of the greatest art and cultural-history museums in the world, was founded in 1746 as the private collection of Catherine II, and gradually accumulated a vast treasury of priceless works of art. It includes valuable collections from the ancient civilizations of Asia, Africa and Europe.

51. Peterhof was the imperial summer palace. Magnificent fountains are an additional attraction of this complex of sumptuous buildings and parks. Built in 1709 by Peter I, it was razed to the ground by bombing in World War II, but was completely reconstructed in 1944 (pp. 90—91).

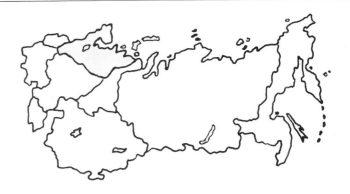

Treasury of Russian Art
The European North

Kiev, Novgorod and Vladimir: this triangle formed the nucleus of the old Russia. Slavery played no part in Russia's development: like medieval West European countries, it evolved as a feudal society, with agriculture as the basis of its economy.

At first the 'smerdi', as Russians called farmers, were free and paid tribute only to their rulers, the princes. However, the princes and their vassals (the boyars) gradually became large landowners and the independence of the smerdi was steadily eroded.

The first mention of the old Kiev-Novgorod state dates from the ninth century. However, eastern Slavs appeared here much earlier and started building their first settlements on the right bank of the Dnieper. The migration of the Slavs lasted several centuries: northwards to the Arctic Ocean, southwards to the Danube and eastwards to the Oka, a tributary of the Volga. The Slavs worked the land with primitive tools — wooden plows, sickles, scythes, axes.

They were still pagans, worshiping the forces of nature and offering sacrifices to their gods: the sun god Dazhbog, the god of cattle and trade Veles, the god of fire and crafts Svarog, the god of thunder and war Perun. By sacrificing to their deities the best of what they had — food, cattle, slaves — they hoped to survive and preserve their wealth.

The Russian north played an important role in the destiny of the country from ancient times. A thousand years ago there were ancient towns here — Staraya Russa, Ladoga, Torzhok, Korela, Oreshek and the largest and most beautiful, Novgorod and Pskov.

All these towns and dozens of others governed the vast expanses of land which surrounded them. In the south, the frontier followed the line of the rivers which flowed northwards to the basins of the Western Dvina and Volga rivers; in the west it extended as far as Finland, in the east to the slopes of the Urals, and in the north to the Polar Circle and the Arctic islands. The natural center of this territory which stretches 2000 kilometers from west to east and 1500 from north to south, was the town of Novgorod, one of the oldest in Russia. It is mentioned in a late tenth-century chronicle as the second most important city of Kievan Rus. In the early feudal times (12th—15th c.) Novgorod was the capital of a principality, widely renowned for its excellent craftsmen and traders. The Dvina region was famed for its beavers and martins, the Pechorski district for ermine and polar fox and the Yugra area for sable. Squirrels were so numerous that tens of thousands of skins were sold each year. Squirrel pelts were also used as a means of payment.

Novgorod, which at first was subordinate to Kiev, grew up on the banks of the Volkhov river, at a crossroads important not only for Russia, but for northern Europe as well. The fact that it stood at the junction of routes 'from

52. The interior of the Cathedral of St Isaac, one of the masterpieces of Russian Classicism. The great dome, 21 meters in diameter, is decorated with statues and frescoes. The interior is covered with malachite and several kinds of marble.

Varangia to Greece', certainly promoted the development of crafts and commerce.

The route from 'Varangia to Greece' connected northern Russia with the southern, the Baltic and Scandinavia with Byzantium. This waterway began to be used in the late ninth century. Already in the eleventh century there were streets in Novgorod which bore names according to the occupation of the inhabitants: tanners, blacksmiths, ironmongers, shieldmakers and others. The twelfth century saw the formation of the first merchant corporation. Trade flourished and goods from Flanders and German towns crossed paths with those from Constantinople and Astrakhan. This brought Novgorod much wealth and merchants were highly respected.

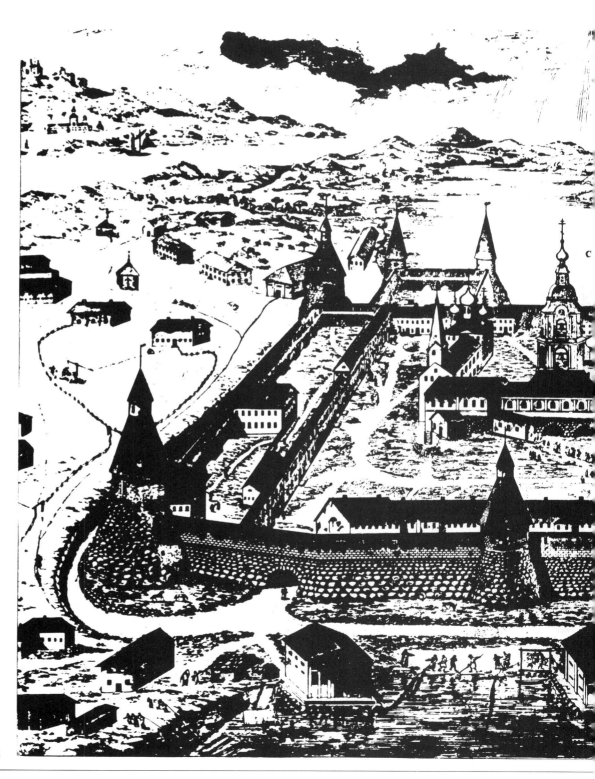

Solovets Monastery, engraving, 18th c.

Varangians was the Slav name for the Vikings. The waterway from the Varangians to the Greeks went from the Gulf of Finland, along the Neva river, across Lake Lagoda and down the Volkhov river. The ships were then transported overland to the Dnieper and continued sailing to Byzantium via the Black Sea.

Old Novgorod was a famous center of Russian culture and art. Being one of the few towns which had not been ruined or burnt down during the campaigns of the Mongol-Tartar hordes, over the centuries it not only preserved but multiplied its cultural monuments and wealth. After becoming part of the centralized Russian state (1478), Novgorod remained one of the country's most important economic centers until the eighteenth century. With

Kizhi. Village graveyard. Engraving by R. Zotov, 1812.

35,000 inhabitants and over 5000 houses, in 1546 Novgorod was the third biggest town after Moscow and Pskov. Proof of the town's size and significance can be found in chronicles which record that as many as 1500 little shops were located in its commercial quarter and that over 200 crafts and trades were practiced.

Novgorod suffered most during the war with Sweden in the early seventeenth century. Between 1611 and 1617 its population fell to only 8000 but its finest buildings were unharmed.

Today there are 62 exceptional works of architecture in Novgorod, raised between the eleventh and eighteenth centuries. The Kremlin (fortress) with its walls and towers from the fifteenth and seventeenth centuries has also been preserved. The Cathedral of St Sophia, the most famous monument of early Russian architecture, built between 1045 and 1050, stands within the Kremlin walls. Even today there is a folk saying: "Where St Sophia is, there is Novgorod, too."

Among the major cultural monuments is the Granitovaya Palace (1433), the Bell Tower (1436), the Clock Tower (1443), and in the center of this ensemble, the Russian Millennary Monument, raised in 1862.

Opposite the Kremlin, on the right bank of the Volkhov river, are many old churches: the St Nicholas Cathedral (1113—1136), the Church of St Paraskeva (1120), the St Anthony Cathedral (1117—1119), and St George Cathedral (1119). In some of these, frescoes by Theophanes the Greek and his pupils can be found.

Novgorod is connected with the most important written source of the history of Russian lands, and the Novgorod principality in particular. This is the *Novgorod Chronicles*, which has two versions. The older is preserved in the form of a parchment manuscript from the thirteenth to fourteenth centuries.

The Novgorod Law Charter, a codex of regulations from the fifteenth century preserved in manuscript form, contains much information about legal and property relations in those times.

Some letters, notes and drawings on birch bark, used by ordinary citizens instead of parchment, have also survived. Among these are love poems, drawings, IOUs, invitations to feasts, and wills — all of them written on the bark of birches, trees which symbolize the vast expanses of the Russian north. One of the oldest of these documents, dating from the twelfth century, is about a law suit.

Among the treasures of Russian art are Novgorod's famous fourteenth-century frescoes, although the flourishing of wall-painting was not confined to this city. Novgorod felt the influence of the first, powerful waves of the Renaissance and the renewed interest in the art of antiquity, not only in Italy, but also in Byzantium, Serbia and the Transcaucasus (Zakavkazye). Detailed comparison of some Novgorod frescoes with Venetian ones, especially those in the Church of St Mark, show many similarities, and not only in subject-matter.

Theophanes the Greek, the great artist of his age, played a significant part in the development of painting in Novgorod in the fourteenth century. Theophanes decorated with frescoes forty stone churches throughout Russia in the thirty years that he lived here.

In the thirteenth century the first Novgorod Lives of Saints were written. These are typical hagiographic works about the lives of certain figures canonized by the Orthodox Church. It is interesting that some personalities described in the Novgorod Lives were not canonized until several hundred years later. This, for example, was the case with Bishop Arcadius, whose Life dates from the thirteenth century, but who was proclaimed a saint only in 1549.

The 'younger brother' of Novgorod is Pskov, founded in the twelfth century at the junction of two rivers, the Pskova and Velika. It served as a frontier stronghold of Novgorod, on the far northwestern border of Russia. The importance and role of Pskov increased in the mid-thirteenth century, when the hordes of Batu Khan, Genghis Khan's grandson, swept into Europe. For three years Batu Khan warred in Russia (1237—1239), bringing almost all the towns under his rule. The exceptions were Novgorod and Pskov, possibly because the Mongols preferred to avoid traversing the marshlands surrounding them.

The preservation of the independence of these towns was extremely important, as a section of the Slav population from the principalities under Mongol-Tartar rule took refuge in Novgorod and Pskov. This marked the beginning of a new wave of settlement of the Russian north, which spread at first along the valleys of the North Dvina and Pechora and then further, towards Lake Ladoga and the White Sea. This was, in fact, the second great wave of migration, after that of the eleventh century.

Kholmogorsk carving on bone.

As a military stronghold, Pskov resisted many attacks by German, Lithuanian, Swedish and Polish princes. In the mid-thirteenth century, it survived twenty-six Lithuanian sieges, causing it to be spoken of as a town hard to conquer. The 'Pskov Defence' (1581—1582) is famous in military theory: a Polish army of 70,000 surrounded the city garrisoned by only 30,000 men, who nevertheless succeeded in repelling thirty-one Polish assaults. After a siege of several months, a ten-year peace was signed.

Some distance from Pskov smaller fortifications, often monasteries, were raised. One of them was the Pskov-Pechorski, which still stands today. The walls with nine towers, the main bell tower from 1523, the Church of the Benediction (1541) and the seventeenth-century treasury, have all been preserved. A two-hundred-meter-long cave, a kind of Orthodox catacomb, served as the monastery burial place.

The migration to the north was followed by the colonization of the local population. In the fourteenth century one of the main centers of this coloniza-

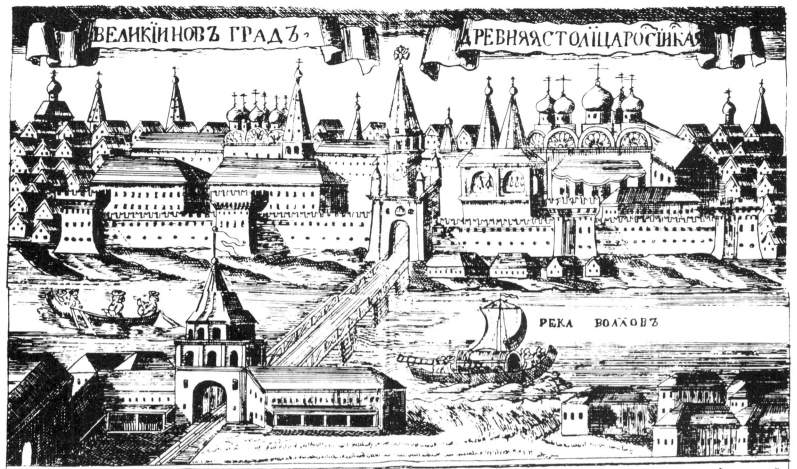

ВЕЛИКİИНОВЪ ГРАДЪ   ДРЕВНЯЯСТОЛİЦАРОСİİКА

РЕКА ВОЛХОВЪ

Внемже попрошенію россіанъ пріиде ЁваряГЬ велнйіи инаЗь рюрнІЬ
его игорь юнй сынъ иданъ дыстьнасоблюдьнівдаде ево Ёлгё Ткна
анрь и поидоша нонієпъ егда иже пришедъ сташинедошедъ їнёпаїпопе
инаждёте и поживанъ мъ игорь сеи жилѣанигьппоййіхъв удити, втолѣ
женіе етдаже просіо россіовсатие' преществіемъ тогда инняЗь влад имерь даде
удіеніасоптопошка обынёов

и инажилъ внелѣ 17 лѣтпъ ну мре послѣ и его оснаси сынъ
жмли вийпъ īу слышеша сано вйкъ пе кнажествойюйтъ Ёсюад и
лъ олегъ прівати исевъ Ёснол асиидпрои иреченмъ почто чождилмъ
престолъ пренесенъ дысть бнопаградазиковъ сановъ грядъ Ёстока и
сё пелиши новъгрё воинажсиіе ейсаоелъ каросашивъ нина жилъ внемъдо

Novgorod, one of the oldest Russian
towns, was the second most important
town of Kievan Rus as early as the
tenth century. Built on the banks of the
Volkhova river, it was a main stop of
the trade route which connected the
north of Europe to Greece and the
Black Sea. It was called Great
Novgorod for its beauty and
magnificent churches.

tion was Velikiy Ustyug, the birthplace, in 1345, of Stephen of Perm. In 1379, as an Orthodox priest, he set off northward to spread Christianity to the Komi peninsula, where the indigenous Ziryani lived. Stephen of Perm's activities contributed to this area becoming part of the grand principality of Muscovy. Stephen created the first alphabet for the Ziryan people, as the Komi were formerly called.

Advancing northward, the settlers built towns, usually around churches. Thus, in the first half of the fifteenth century, the famous Solovietskiy Monastery, one of the largest in Russia, was built on the shore of Solovietskiy Island in the White Sea. Over the next hundred years it expanded its domains, developed crafts and trade, and became the economic and political center of the whole White Sea area.

Most of the monks were engaged in various occupations (hunting, fishing, iron smelting, etc.). The head of the monastery, the archimandrite, was appointed directly by the tsar and the patriarch in Moscow, making it independent in relation to the local princes. Its special privileged status became apparent at the time of the schism in Russia, in the seventeenth century, when the Solovietskiy Monastery opposed Church reform and rebelled against Patriarch Nikon (1668—1676).

The uprising, in which 450—500 monks took part, started under the battlecry "For the Old Faith". Tsar Aleksei Mikhailovich sent troops against the monastery in 1668, but the monks fortified it and refused to admit the soldiers. The siege lasted seven years and only the treason of a monk allowed the army to enter the monastery and crush the rebellion. Of the five hundred monks, only sixty survived and they were later punished.

A powerful fortress (the walls were seven meters thick and ten meters high) with many towers, cannons and a strong garrison, Solovietskiy Monastery became a place of exile for opponents of imperial and church government from the sixteenth century on.

The monastery is an exceptional work of Russian architecture, in which the enormous Cathedral of the Transfiguration (1556—1564) occupies the central place. Many old books and manuscripts have been preserved here. Learned monks who spread Christianity wrote the *Solovietskiy Chronicle*.

Towards the end of the sixteenth century, at the mouth of the North Dvina and near the Archangel Michael Monastery, a new town, Archangel (Arkhangelsk), arose and soon became the main sea port of Muscovite Russia. An important trade route between Archangel and Moscow was established along the North Dvina and Sukhoni rivers. Caravans traveled along it in summer in boats, in winter on sleighs. Merchandise from various West European countries were transported south from the port, along with fish and salt, walrus tusks, and furs from Pechora and the Urals. From the south came wheat, wax, linen, honey . . .

The route led across Lake Onyezhko, where on the island of Kizhi a unique complex of wooden buildings was raised in the seventeenth century. The villages, scattered over the many islands, were administratively united, with Spassk-Kizhi as the center, in the fourteenth century. By the sixteenth, over a hundred villages had been united, and in the seventeenth the construction of a fort for defense against Swedish and Lithuanian-Polish attacks was begun on the central island.

The silhouettes of the wooden churches, built by unknown Russian architects, recall a fairytale scene. It is probably for this reason that Kitezh, which has most of them, was called a 'fairytale town'. This is the setting of the Church of the Transfiguration (1714) with its twenty-two domes, on which the play of light and shadow was exploited to the full. Like the Church of the Intercession with nine domes (1764), it fits perfectly into the natural surroundings, displaying the plasticity of old Russian architecture and confirming the high reputation of its builders. All these churches, bell-towers and domes were built of wood. The prominent painter and historian Igor Grabar described the Transfiguration Church as 'an incomparable fantasy of domes'.

In Kizhi the legend of the architect of this church lives on. When he completed the building, he threw his axe into Lake Onezh saying:

"This church was raised by the master-builder Nestor. None such has ever existed, nor ever will."

And truly, there is no such church anywhere else in Russia. For this reason the people say that it is 'as holy as a hymn'.

The Russian north, which in time became the frontline of Russia's defense, with a chain of impregnable fortified towns (Izborsk, Pskov, Novgorod, Solovka, Koporya, Archangel, Vologda, and others), played an important role in the history of its people by preserving and fostering the traditional spirit of Russian culture, art and folklore. This is understandable, since the southern and central parts of the country had been exposed for several centuries to Mongol-Tartar influences, reflected, among other things, in their culture and art. The famous Russian fairy tales which originated in Kievan Rus were not recorded in either Kiev or Moscow, and would have

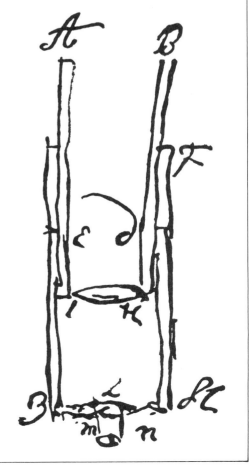

Drawing by V. M. Lomonosov — a design for a telescope for night-time observation.

been lost to us had they not been transmitted by word of mouth in the Russian north.

The north also kept alive many Russian folk sayings and proverbs, described by writer Mikhail Sholokhov as the 'winged wisdom' of the people which 'flies from generation to generation'. Vladimir Dal, who towards the end of the last century collected 30,000 proverbs, recorded two thirds directly among the people, noting down the sayings which peasants used almost daily in their speech.

The north also honors the memory of the greatest Russian poet, Alexander Pushkin (1799—1837). The place where he was buried, Svytogorsk Monastery in the Pskov district, is today called Pushkinska gora. This is a monument under state protection, visited every year by hundreds of thousands of poetry lovers from all over the country, as well as many poets who read their own verse here. Close by is the village of Mikhailovskoye, to which Pushkin was exiled in 1824 for 'anti-government and anti-religious ideas'. It is here that Pushkin wrote the drama *Boris Godunov*, and worked on the novel *Eugene Onegin*, which the critics have called an 'encyclopedia of Russian life' of that time. In Mikhailovskoye, which is also under state protection, Pushkin wrote over one hundred poems which have been included in anthologies of the greatest Russian and world poetry.

In the Svyatogorsk Monastery, the spot where Pushkin's coffin stood is specially marked, and a death mask of the famous poet is placed beside it.

Another famous protected corner of the Russian north is Staraya Russa. Under the name Rusha it is well known as one of the oldest Slav settlements (6th c.), founded according to legend by the warrior Rus.

Staraya Russa has several buildings of great historic and artistic value. These are the Church of the Transfiguration (1198), which has some twelfth-century paintings, and the Church of St George (early 15th c.), with a seventeenth-century iconostasis that is considered the model of Russian woodcarving.

Staraya Russa is also a well-known health resort where Fyodor Dostoevski stayed and underwent medical treatment from time to time. It was here that he wrote his *Brothers Karamazov*.

53. The isolated wooden churches in the north bear testimony to the great distances over which Christianity spread during the conversion of Russia. These churches, whose builders are mostly unknown, are outstanding examples of popular creativity.

54. Lakes and mountains — a typical view in the Kola peninsula. Although far north, its coastal towns were long the main trading ports connecting Russia with Europe and the world. Trade contributed to the relatively rapid development of northern Russia in the twelfth to fifteenth centuries, when timber, fur, leather and precious stones began to be exported (pp. 102—103).

55. Novgorod is first mentioned in a chronicle from 859, the year which is taken as its date of foundation. Over several centuries Novgorod played a major role in Russian history. Because it was spared Tartar destruction, many of its medieval buildings have been preserved to the present day (pp. 104—105).

Drawing of an ancient church in the margin of the Pskov Typikon, 12th c.

56. Detail of an icon depicting Ivan
III's campaign against Novgorod. In the
decisive battle fought in July 1741, the
Novgorodians suffered a bitter defeat
and thus lost their independence of
the central government in Moscow.

57

57. The Millennary Monument was
unveiled in Novgorod in 1862 to
commemorate 1,000 years of the state
of Russia. The work of M. O. Mekishin,
it depicts, among other things, 129
figures of the greatest Russian
statesmen, scientists and artists.

58. The early Russian settlements in
the north were built on the banks of
rivers and lakes. The church, usually
wooden, was raised in the center of
the village, as a symbol of the
communal spiritual life of the local
population (pp. 108—109).

59

59—60. The history of Novgorod is intertwined with that of Kizhi, since this is where settlers from Novgorod raised their first villages, on the banks of Lake Onega. The earliest chronicles mentioning churches with pointed domes date from the sixteenth century. The most famous are those dedicated to the Transfiguration (1714) with its twenty-two domes, and the Intercession (1764) with its tall, pointed bell-tower. These unusual buildings were constructed without using a single nail. The complex of churches in Kizhi was completed in 1784.

The Baltic Republics
Estonia, Lithuania, Latvia

Amber, the 'treasure of the Baltic', can be found in many countries, but nowhere else in such abundance: the Baltic area is thought to contain ninety percent of the world's reserves of this 'stone'. The inhabitants of the Baltic republics, Latvia, Lithuania and Estonia, are taught in school that their amber, 'the purest in the world', is between 35 and 140 million years old.

Amber comes from the resin of ancient pines which flowed down the trunks whenever the bark was scratched, and collected in lumps on the ground. Twigs, leaves, flowers, insects and anything else borne by the wind stuck to the fresh resin and disintegrated. Over millions of years, the extensive forests of the region produced huge quantities of this resin, which became petrified under the earth or sea and turned into amber.

As amber is only slightly heavier than water, it is often thrown up on the shore during storms. The largest piece, found in 1860, weighed almost ten kilograms.

The Lithuanian town of Palanga has the only amber museum in the world. Lithuanian craftsmen have long been famed for their treatment of amber: some dedicate their whole lives to cutting it and bringing out its hidden beauty. Amber is divided into five categories according to the degree of clarity and color, which ranges from pale yellow to dark red.

Today amber may have lost its former value — in ancient Rome, for example, it was worth its weight in gold — but even today it is irreplaceable in the production of the highest quality varnish, certain apparatus and instruments and, certainly, in the production of jewelry. The great palace raised by the Empress Elizabeth at Tsarskoye Selo (today Pushkin) near Leningrad, once had a world-famous amber room of fabulous value. Unfortunately, all the amber disappeared during the Second World War and has never been traced.

The Soviet Pribaltika lies in the northwest of the country, its three little republics almost 'tucked into' Western Europe. Hemmed in between powerful states, during their thousand-year history, the peoples of the Pribaltika, despite all their differences in origins and language, have had one thing in common: a history of wars, battles and conflicts with their mighty neighbors.

The population of these republics are the descendants of the peoples which inhabited these areas several thousand years ago. The Lithuanian nation, for example, originates from two kindred peoples with related languages — Lithuanians and Zhmuds (Samogitians). This distinction has survived to the present day. The Latvians or Letts, on the other hand, were formed by the fusion of several different ethnic groups: the Semigallians, Selonians, Latgalians and indigenous Kurs. Soviet scholars have demon-

61. This iconostasis in Kizhi was painted by self-taught artists, their names now unknown. However, the compositions, color and spiritual power of the Kizhi altar still arouse our admiration.

strated the closeness of the forefathers of the Balts and the Slavs, which is also borne out by the similarity of their languages.

The Estonians or Ests, whose language belongs to the Finno-Ugrian group, were divided as early as the beginning of the thirteenth century. The northern part of their territory was occupied by the Danes, who in 1219 built the stronghold of Ravel, called by the Ests Tallinn, meaning 'Danish town'. Tallinn is today the capital of the Soviet Republic of Estonia. The southern part of the old Ests' homeland was captured at the end of the twelfth century by German crusaders, who subsequently became rulers of Latvian and Lithuanian territories as well.

The German Knights — whose associations bore picturesque names such as the Livonian Order, Teutonic Order, Order of the Knights of the Sword —

Conversion of Lithuanians, engraving, 1572.

subdued the greater part of the Pribaltika and founded their German feudal state. The occupation of the Baltic seaboard is seen by historians in a broader context: as part of the crusades to the East.

The German crusaders brought Christianity with them. As early as 1201, Riga, today the capital of Latvia, was the seat of a German bishop, and the construction of the first Christian churches began soon after.

For over two hundred years the Lithuanians warred against the German Ritters. Between 1340 and 1410 alone the Teutonic and Livonian knights attacked Lithuanian princes almost one hundred times. Towards the end of the fourteenth century the Lithuanians and Poles joined forces, and in 1410 this new union won a decisive victory in the battle of Grunwald (Tannenberg). With the power of the German Knights broken, Lithuania was no longer subjected to incessant attacks from the west.

The destiny of the Estonians was similar. In the thirteenth century part of their lands was occupied by Germans and Danes, and in the fourteenth, the Danish crown sold part of the Estonian land to the Teutonic Order of Knights (1346). Some 120 years later, Estonia fell under Swedish rule, and after the Great Northern War came under the sovereignty of Russia (1721).

Vilnius, drawing, 1550.

Engraving from the book "Description of European Sarmatia", 1583.

The history of the Pribaltika is also recorded in stone, in the appearance of the old towns of Riga (Latvia), Tallinn (Estonia), Vilnius (Lithuania) and others. Architecturally, these cities differ from other Russian towns. Their narrow streets with neat little houses, churches in the Gothic style and city squares and parks bear a closer resemblance to some small German towns.

Riga, first mentioned in 1201, joined the Hanseatic League some years later, thus acquiring a monopoly in trade with Novgorod, Smolensk, Vitebsk and other principalities. Riga — also the name of a winding little river — is a real mercantile city to which traders not only from the Baltic, but also from Russia and even Constantinople, used to come to do business.

Old Riga, dominated by the Romanesque and Gothic styles, has over eighty buildings of major historical-cultural value. One of the oldest churches is St Peter's, first mentioned in 1209. It was damaged and set alight many times during the wars, and in 1721 lightning struck its wooden dome, which was destroyed by fire together with the interior. The rebuilding of the church, ordered by Peter I, was completed in 1746. At that time it was the tallest wooden structure in the world (120 meters).

One of the most beautiful architectural monuments in Riga is the Domkirk. This great cathedral, first built in 1211, was reconstructed and restored many times up to the end of the last century. The oldest part is the capitol hall in the Romanesque style. The Gothic gallery which encloses the inner court on three sides is also greatly admired. The brick tower, some 90 meters tall, was completed in 1776.

The Domkirk, now a museum and concert hall, has a very large and valuable organ, with 6700 pipes and 127 registers, which was built and installed in 1883. The concert hall is considered one of the most acoustic in the world.

The Ekaba Church, also from the early thirteenth century, is another notable building in Riga. After the victory of the Reformation in the sixteenth century, it housed the first Latvian school. The Ekaba Church, 80 meters tall, has retained its sixteenth-century appearance.

A particularly interesting architectural ensemble stands on the bank of the Daugava (Dvina) river, the site of one of the most important fortresses. The castle, begun in 1330, was ruined during the wars of the following century. In the early sixteenth century it was rebuilt, but as a result of subsequent reconstruction and alteration, only its foundations have been preserved to the present day. At the corners of the square building two large round domes were raised diagonally opposite each other, and two small square cupolas. During the later alterations, the castle lost its original medieval appearance. The White Hall was built after the Napoleonic War, and the Red Hall in the early twentieth century.

Riga has preserved many picturesque narrow streets, a reminder of past centuries. Some of these, in which the widely acclaimed craftsmen had their shops, are only two meters wide and are now used only by pedestrians. Craft shops can still be found here, their appearance unchanged over the centuries. No. 17 Maza Pils Street is a typical Riga merchant's house from the fifteenth century. When it was built, only one room was planned for domestic purposes, while the upstairs chambers were used for storage. The Danenstern house, built in 1696 in typical Baroque style, is an exceptional architectural undertaking. The five stories which housed merchandise were connected with a kind of lift, or rather a windlass, by means of which the goods were raised to the upper floors.

Vilnius, the capital of Lithuania, was founded in 1323 by Grand Prince Gediminas. Archeological excavations have shown, however, that there was a settlement on this site as early as the fifth century BC. Vilnius, also called

Wilno, was the capital of the grand principality of Lithuania until 1569 (the Lublin Union with Poland). Like other similar towns, the city had its own local government, which fostered not only the speedy development of trade and crafts, but the flourishing of the arts.

In early 1525, the Belorussian printer Francisk Skorina set up a press in Vilnius and printed the book *The Apostle*. Somewhat later the Mamonich brothers also established a press and published a number of works. These were printed in Belorussian at first; it was not until the end of the sixteenth century that Canon M. Dauksha translated the Catechism, and later other texts, into Lithuanian. In about 1560 the first Lithuanian primer was printed. In

1578 an academy teaching theology and philosophy was founded in Vilnius *A tavern, engraving, 1500.*
by the Order of Jesus. Around the mid-eighteenth century, lectures in physics,
political science, mathematics and geology were introduced, and in 1773 the
academy was renamed the Main School of Lithuania, which later grew into
the University (1803).

Vilnius, the center of a small state which was constantly at war, also built
many fortresses, at first of wood, but later of stone. The latter, preserved to
this day, have massive, virtually impregnable, stone walls, their architecture
being entirely subordinated to military-strategic needs. In the fifteenth
century, however, towns in which the central area was reserved for trade and

workshops started to develop. At about the same time the Catholic Church started its own building activity, mostly in the Gothic style. In the sixteenth century Lithuanian architecture adopted some of the ideas of the Italian Renaissance and this style flourished side by side with the traditional Gothic, giving Lithuanian towns a specific charm. Castle Radvilu in Biržai, from the late sixteenth and early seventeenth centuries, is a typical example of the infuence of Italian architecture.

Vilnius and other old towns of the republic, such as Kaunas, have many sumptuous Baroque buildings. Apart from local craftsmen, in the early seventeenth century foreign architects were also employed — Italians, Germans and others. Some churches in Vilnius (for example the Church of St Kazimir) look as though they have doubles in distant Rome.

In the late eighteenth and early nineteenth centuries some fine Classical buildings were raised in Vilnius, such as the Cathedral of St Stanislav — today an art gallery. This mixture of architectural styles makes a walk through this beautiful town a stroll through history and past centuries.

Tallinn, the capital of Estonia, was called Ravel until 1917. It is first mentioned in writings of the Arab geographer Idris in 1154, and is referred to in Russian chronicles as Kolivan (the town of Kaleva, hero of a folk epic). The name Ravel was given to the town by the Danes, who captured it in 1219, but to the Estonians it was Tallinn even then (Taani linna = Danish town or fortress).

In the mid-thirteenth century Tallinn entered the German Hanseatic League. In the following centuries, although it enjoyed a period of independent and prosperous development, Tallinn fell from time to time under the rule of neighboring countries, and from 1561 was governed by the Swedes. The Russian army laid siege to the city in 1570, 1571 and 1577, but failed to capture it.

During the period of Swedish rule, manufacturing started to develop. The first press was set up in 1634, and a year later a paper-mill began production. In 1631 a high school was founded.

Between the wars, the fate of the three Baltic seaboard states was similar. Under the influence of the October Revolution (1917), social unrest spread through Estonia, Lithuania and Latvia. Soviets of workers' and soldiers' deputies took power, and soon a new, soviet government was proclaimed. In Tallinn, for example, this took place only one day after the October Revolution in Russia (November 8).

All this, however, was short-lived. In February of the following year, the Kaiser's army marched in and Estonia was proclaimed an independent 'bourgeois' republic in November 1918. The course of events in the other two states was similar.

Between the two world wars, Estonia, Lithuania and Latvia were formally independent states, although under strong German influence. Since 1939 they have been part of the USSR, in which they have enjoyed the reputation of being the most developed republics.

62.   A typical street in the old part of Tallinn, where the charm of late medieval European urban architecture can still be felt. Tallinn's former name, Ravel, was given by the Danes after they captured it in 1219. Ravel was one of the leading Hanseatic towns in the Middle Ages.

63.   The castle of Trakai, raised in 1541, served for a time as the residence of Lithuanian grand princes. Now fully restored, it again shines in all its former magnificence (pp. 122—123).

64. Riga, the capital of Latvia, is one of the oldest towns of the Pribaltika. First mentioned by this name in the thirteenth century, it was once the largest port on the eastern shore of the Baltic Sea. Because of its cosmopolitan atmosphere and mixed ethnic composition, between the two world wars Riga was called the 'Paris of the North'. Today it is still a major scientific, cultural and economic center.

65. In Riga, a city with an old-world atmosphere, there are no longer as many chimneys as there used to be. The chimneysweep's trade, however, is still respected, both as a necessity of everyday life and as a part of tradition.

66. Vilnius, or Vilna, the capital of Lithuania, was founded in 1128. When Grand Prince Gediminas moved his capital here in the fifteenth century, the city began to develop rapidly as a center of trade and crafts. In 1579 a university was founded in this town.

67. The City Library, a landmark of Vilnius, houses rare editions from the fifteenth to eighteenth centuries in various languages, as well as a large collection of manuscripts and music literature.

68. The Domkirk, built in the early thirteenth century as the cathedral church of the archbishop of Riga, has retained its original appearance to the present day. It contains one of the finest organs in the world, on which leading organists frequently give recitals of works by Bach, Handel and other composers. The stained-glass windows give the interior a special atmosphere, creating a harmony of light and sound.

69. The Baltic peoples cherish their culture and folklore. For centuries exposed to powerful conquerors and cultural assimilation, they have succeeded in preserving a high level of national awareness and cultural autonomy.

70—71.   The traditional annual 'Song Festival', brings together dozens of choirs and thousands of singers from all parts of Estonia. The program attracts great public interest and tens of thousands of visitors. The famous Estonian folklore scholar Gustav Ernesaks has been the festival's director for a number of years.

72.   Sea, sun and stone: Baltic nature in a concentrated form, outdoing anything that art can create.

The Cradle of the State
The Ukraine, Moldavia, the Crimea

The southern European part of Russia is the cradle of its statehood. According to legend, Kiev, the largest city in southern Russia, was founded by three brothers (Kiv, Shchek and Khoriv) and their sister (Libed), and named after the eldest brother.

Archeological finds indicate that the settlement was established in the second half of the fifth century. By the eighth or ninth it had become a leading center of crafts and trade and the capital of the old Russian state — Kievan Rus.

The name 'Ukraina' at first denoted a border territory and as such was applied to the frontier region southwest of Russia. In time its meaning changed, and by the sixteenth century the name was used in official documents for all the united lands of the Ukraine. Somewhat earlier (14th—15th c.), the Ukrainians are mentioned as an independent Slav ethnic group with their own language, culture and territories, i.e. as a separate nationality from the Russians.

At first Kiev was a frontier stronghold of the East Slavs against nomadic warriors from the steppes. Between 882 and 1224 Russia was constantly under attack, first by the Vikings from the north, and later, when the Slavs moved south and east, by Mongol-Tartar hordes. Thus Kiev, too, often fell to foreigners.

Chronicles mention that in the ninth century there were over twenty East Slav towns in which crafts and trade flourished, Kiev being one of them. This was the period of the formation of small feudal states, principalities. The first known princes of Kievan Rus were Askold and Dir, followed by Oleg, who ruled from 879—912. The golden age of Kievan Rus was the reign of Prince Vladimir (980—1015), when Russia adopted Christianity.

According to written documents, in 988 Prince Vladimir, having previously become convinced of the falsity of pagan gods, decided to convert to Christianity. After conducting a whole series of investigations, negotiations and even military campaigns, he acknowledged Byzantine Orthodoxy as the one true faith. After Vladimir's conversion, all his subjetcs were duly baptized on his orders.

However, even the church historian Golubinski was later bold enough to confess his belief that all the accounts in the chronicles and Life of Vladimir concerning the acceptance of Christianity as the state religion were 'well-intentioned inventions', based on various Byzantine stories, and contained no truth except the fact itself that in 988 or 989 Vladimir and his court adopted the Byzantine Orthodox faith, which was proclaimed the official religion.

Some Russian historians claim that some fifty years before the official conversion, there was a church in Kiev dedicated to St Elijah, where Christians practiced their religion. Most of the population, however, worshipped

73. The streets of old Tallinn resemble German towns. The street lighting, such as was used a century ago, lends the old part of town a particular charm.

Self-portrait of Francisco Skorin, 16th-c. Belorussian publisher and educator.

Perun, the supreme god of the Slav pagan pantheon.

In *The Tale of Bygone Times*, in the so-called Primary Russian Chronicle, the account of the 'conversion of Russia' contains a number of contradictions, and even different dates are mentioned. It is said that Prince Vladimir was undecided as to which religion to adopt. First of all, in 986 Moslems from Volgan Bulgaria came to him, followed by Jews from the Khazarian lands, and finally Christians from Rome and Byzantium. They all had their own proposals as to which religion the prince of Kievan Rus should adopt.

At the time when Vladimir became a Christian, a large number of his troops had already converted to the new faith. There were certainly political reasons as well for the adoption of Byzantine Christianity, and the fact that Prince Vladimir had married the sister of the Byzantine emperor was an additional reason for his acceptance of this faith.

Since most of the inhabitants of Kievan Rus were forcibly baptized, in order to make everything more convincing and clear to the ordinary people, Vladimir ordered that all the pagan idols, to which they had prayed and offered sacrifices, be thrown into the Dnieper river. Whether based on historical fact or legend, there is still a belief that Prince Vladimir carried a statue of Perun through Kiev in a ritual procession, tossed it into the Dnieper, and then compelled thousands of people to immerse themselves in the river, wash themselves and accept Christianity.

New priests came together with the new religion from Byzantium, and Metropolitan Michael (Mikhail), who in Constantinople had been named the first head of the Russian Orthodox Church, was installed in Kiev. The Byzantine clergy soon traveled as far as Novgorod, Rostov and other ancient cities, propagating the new faith. This was a difficult task to start with: it is said that 'Putyaga converted Novgorod by the sword, Dobrinya by fire'. The first two bishops fled from Rostov, the people rose against the third, Leontius, and it was only the fourth bishop, Isaiah, who managed to burn all the pagan idols and convert the population with the aid of the army.

Christianity in Russia, which celebrated its millennium in 1988, at first developed in a kind of symbiosis with the old cults, leading some historians to speak of elements of 'dual faith' as a specifically Russian phenomenon. Some old cults, such as those of Dionysus, Pan and other deities, survived within the framework of the new religion, albeit in somewhat different forms. The cult of Dionysus, for example, was replaced by that of St George (georgos = farmer). It was advised that new places of worship should be raised on the sites of old Dionysian temples, ancient rites were used for their inaugura-

Fragment of decoration on the staircase of the Cathedral of St Sophia.

tion and even sacrifices made. The clergy preached that there were angels with 'special functions' — angels of the hills and rivers, oxen and sheep, thunder and hail, frost and sweat, spring and autumn, day and night, victory and happiness — and that every man should have his own guardian angel whom he should venerate. This 'dual faith' was thus a fusion of pagan and Christian beliefs.

The great church historian Nestor, a monk of the Kievan Pecherski Monastery, was the author of *The Tale of Bygone Times* (1113), an exceptionally valuable account of historical events, folklore and legends.

After the 'baptism of Russia', the Slavic Cyrillic alphabet was brought from Macedonia. Books were translated and copied, and Russia gradually became acquainted with religious, literary and historical works, and was introduced to the heritage of ancient Greece, Rome and the Orient. By accepting Christianity, Russia entered the circle of countries which carried on the traditions of classical culture. Moreover, the Church helped unify the various principalites. It spread literacy and with it new concepts of man, culture and the arts, which were developed for centuries in a specific manner by the Orthodox Church.

Scholars have speculated as to why Russia chose Byzantine Christianity as its official religion and not some other. It is true that it could as well have adopted Islam, Judaism or some other faith. The choice of Christianity, in its Orthodox form, was the consequence of both internal needs — Prince Vladimir was searching for an ideology which would help to unite his subjects, whose various tribes each had their own main 'deities', and external factors, above all, the increasingly close trade links with Byzantium.

The culture of Kievan Rus was original and highly developed. The flourishing of architecture in the early eleventh century is best illustrated by the Cathedral of St Sophia and the Golden Gate (1037), the Cathedral of the Assumption (Uspenski Sobor) of the Pecherski Monastery (1073—78), and the Cathedral of the Redeemer (Spasski Sobor) at Chernigov, founded in 1036.

From here originate the old written documents, such as the Ostromir

*Page from the "Kievan Book of Hours",
1617.*

Gospel, *The Tale of Bygone Years, Russian Justice* — the first collection of laws, *The Discourse on Law and Grace* by Metropolitan Ilarion, and other works of the eleventh century. The literary heritage of Kievan Rus and the rich oral folk tradition formed the basis for the appearance of *The Lay of Igor's Campaign,* the most famous work of early Russian literature, in the twelfth century.

Kiev's role declined in the thirteenth century with the advance of the Mongols and Tartars. Like many other towns it was burnt down in 1240, and the Russian principalities came under the sway of the new Mongol-Tartar state of the Golden Horde. The Mongol invasion had lasting economic, social and political consequences. Russian life was greatly impoverished by the destruction of the cities, in which crafts, trade and culture had only just begun to thrive. Although the Mongols soon withdrew once more to the steppes, leaving the Russian lords only the obligation of paying a high tribute, their influence nevertheless continued to be strongly felt. The elimination of the urban class opened the way for a new autocracy which imitated Mongol rule in its ruthless terror and cruelty. This cut short the flowering of Kievan Rus and halted its development for a long time to come.

* * *

The fate of Kiev and of other ancient cities on the territory of the present-day Ukraine bears witness to the turbulent history of this central plain, the cradle of the Russian state. In the northeast of the Ukraine, on the right bank of the deep and wide river Seym, lies Putivl, famed as an important fortification of old Russia and the scene of events described in the most celebrated work of old Russian literature, *The Lay of Igor's Campaign.* The ancient town of Putivl was a crossroads of important trade routes which led from Kiev to other cities, north and south.

The present-day town of Zaporozhye in southeastern Ukraine was the site in the twelfth century of the Zaporoshka Secha fortress, where Russian princes gathered before doing battle with the Tartars or fighting the Polovtsi (Kumans). It was from here that they set off toward the river Kalka in 1223, when the Russian army was defeated by the Mongol hordes of Batu Khan.

Southwest of Kiev lies Berdichev with its famous fortresses and towers from the sixteenth century. In 1849, Honoré de Balzac married Eveline Hanska (née Ewelina Rzewuska), and for a time lived on her estate in the nearby village of Verhovnya, where there is now a memorial museum.

By the decision of the Zemski Sobor or Territorial Assembly in Moscow, on October 1, 1658, Russia and the Ukraine were united. A year later this decision was also confirmed by the Pereyaslavska Rada (parliament) in Kiev.

The unification came at a time when the Ukraine was under strong pressure from the north (from the Poles and Lithuanians who had entered into a state union in 1569), as well as from the south and west (frequent attacks by Turks and Tartars from the Crimean Khanate). All this, together with frequent peasant uprisings, seriously weakened the Ukraine, which turned to Russia in its search for a powerful ally. The war against Poland was led by Hetman Bogdan Khelmnitzki.

Under the unification, the Ukraine obtained autonomous status within Russia.

From the ninth to eleventh centuries, Kievan Rus included parts of the present-day Ukraine around the rivers Berezina, Pripyat and Sozh, and the upper course of the Neman. In the south of the Republic stretches the Dnieper-Bug canal. Low hills give way to plains, which gradually turn into the marshes of Polesie.

Cover of "Dead Souls" made by the author, Nikolai Gogol.

Belorussian or White Russian culture is of ancient origin. In the time of Kievan Rus, many buildings famed for their architecture were raised here, among them the Cathedral of St Sophia in Polotsk and the Kolozhska Church in Grodno. Belorussia is noted for its poets and writers, and for the richness of its folklore.

* * *

In the south of the Ukraine lies the famous port of Odessa, on the shores of the Black Sea. The name of the city originated in the mistaken belief that it stood on the site of the ancient Greek colony of Odessos. It is true, however, that various ancient settlements had existed here: Cimmerian, Scythian, Sarmatian, Greek, Slav. In the time of Kievan Rus it was inhabited by East Slav tribes. The settlement from this early period was destroyed in the fifteenth century by the Turks, who raised a new one, named Khadzhibei.

In August 1794 the foundations were laid of the future port of Odessa, today called 'the southern sea gate' of the Soviet Union. The construction of the harbor and city was directed by the famous Russian army commander, A. Suvorov, whom Catherine II entrusted with the building of all forts and military objects. Odessa is one of the few old towns raised according to a plan.

Odessa is a city with a rich cultural tradition, a center of theatrical and literary life. The oldest theater, the Academy Theater of Opera and Ballet, founded in 1809, staged productions starring the famous artists Chaliapin and Sobinov. The year 1817 saw the opening of the Richelieu Lycée, which later grew into a university.

Alexander Pushkin was deported to Odessa in 1823—24, and was inspired by the exotic atmosphere of the port to write *The Fountain of Bakhchisarai* and *Gypsies*.

Later, especially in the early twentieth century, the city was regarded as the literary center of the whole country; Anton Pavlovich Chekhov was among the many literary figures who stayed or lived here.

Odessa is a southern town which stretches along a bay in the shape of an elongated amphitheater. The pride of its inhabitants is the seashore boulevard with its magnificent flights of steps, on which the most dramatic scenes of Sergei Eisenstein's *Battleship Potemkin* were filmed. The Potemkin Steps, constructed by F. Bofo (1837—1841), lead from the harbor up to the central square with a statue of the Duc de Richelieu, governor-general of the region in the early nineteenth century.

The Ukraine is today the largest and economically most important Soviet republic after Russia. With more than fifty million inhabitants, it is now predominantly industrial, but with a strong agriculture. One of the major areas for metalurgy and coal-mining, it produces over 60 million tons of steel annually — more than the Federal Republic of Germany, and large quantities of coal, electricity, coke and chemical fertilizers.

Along the eastern border of the Ukraine lies the republic of Moldavia, extending over 350 kilometers from north to south, and 150 from east to west. Along the river Prut, Moldavia borders on Romania.

This land lay in the path of all invaders throughout history. The Scythians, Greeks, Persians, Romans, Goths, Poles and Swedes all passed through it; it was ravaged by the Turks and burnt by the Tartars. Legends and folk songs tell of the centuries-long suffering, the battles and heroic deeds of this people.

Archeological finds show the area was inhabited 100,000 years ago, at a time when most of Europe was still under ice. Proper settlements were not

Musicians performing. Fragment of decoration on the staircase of the Cathedral of St Sophia.

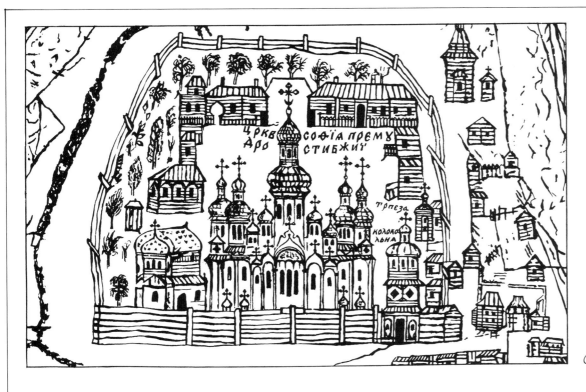

Cathedral of St Sophia, old engraving.

founded, naturally, until much later — about 1000 BC. From this period date the kurgans (burial and watch-guard mounds), many belonging to the Bronze Age.

Towards the middle of the first century BC the Roman Empire started its conquest of the Danubian-Carpathian lands. Dacia, which emerged out of a tribal union of the forefathers of the Moldavians, put up a strong resistance to the Roman legions, but in 106 Emperor Trajan finally subdued them, and many Dacians were slaughtered or enslaved. Dacia became a Roman province and Latin the official language, from which Moldavian and Romanian later developed.

The fall of Rome in the fifth century led to the more rapid settlement of Slav tribes in the region. The oldest Russian chronicle, *The Tale of Bygone Times*, states that the Tivertsi and Uchichi lived between the rivers Prut and Southern Bug. Their intermingling with the romanized population resulted in the formation of the Wallachian (Vlach) tribe, the forefathers of today's Moldavians.

The Moldavian principality, formed in 1359, stretched from the Carpathians to the Black Sea. Bogdan, the first Moldavian ruler recorded in history, is considered to be its founder. Stephen III (1457—1504), also called the Great, was the most powerful of its princes or voivodes. During his reign, he fought against the invading Turks and Tartars and repelled the attacks of Hungarian and Polish kings. In Kishinev, where he is buried, his tomb bears the following inscription: "Brave in danger, strong in suffering, modest in happiness. He aroused the admiration of rulers and the people; he knew how to create great things with little means."

Family ties, but also common interests, brought a Moldavian delegation to Moscow in order to sign an agreement on the entry of Moldavia into Russia. In 1791 a part was ceded to Russia, while the rest of the principality entered into the union two years later. By the treaty of Bucharest (1812), Bessarabia also became a part of Russia.

After World War I Bessarabia was once more Romanian, while Moldavia, as an autonomous province, became part of the Ukraine in 1924. On June 28,

1940, Bessarabia was ceded to the Soviet Union by Romania, forming part of the newly-established Moldavian Republic.

One of the smallest Soviet republics (33,700 square kilometers), Moldavia has some five million inhabitants and is famed for its vine-growing, good wines, vegetables, fruit and corn.

* * *

In the south of the Soviet part of Europe lies the Crimean peninsula, its shores washed by the Black Sea and the Sea of Azov. Nature has been generous to this region of plains and hills, woods and pastures, salt lakes and deep rivers. The mountainous Crimea is in fact a green island in the midst of the vast steppes.

The administrative center of the Crimea is Simferopol, a town in typical southern style, its white-stone buildings set amid lush greenery. Not far from Simferopol stretches the Petrovske steppe, the natural border of the once-powerful Scythian state which existed here from the third century BC to the fourth century AD. On the site of its former capital, Neapolis, whole blocks of buildings are preserved, and many of the objects excavated have been placed in the Scythian museum.

The Crimea, renowned for its healthy climate, has several spas and resorts, of which Yalta is the most famous. Here, before our era, lived the ancient Tauri. During the period of Tartar-Turkish rule it was a mere fishing village, but in the eighteenth century Russian rulers started distributing the best land here to their courtiers and Tartar vassal lords. At nearby Livadia, where the tsar's summer residence was located, many other magnificent villas sprang up, and Yalta became a fashionable gathering place of the Russian and foreign nobility.

It was at Livadia that Churchill, Roosevelt and Stalin met to discuss the fate of the world at the Yalta Conference, near the end of World War II.

Not far from Yalta is Bakhchisarai, once the capital of the Crimean Khanate. The royal palace (16th—18th c.), is well preserved, and today houses a museum.

74. A view of Kiev from Vladimir Hill. According to legend, in 988 'the light of Christ's faith' shone over Kiev, inspiring the Kievan prince, Vladimir, to adopt the new religion — Christianity. Kiev is mentioned as a Russian frontier stronghold as early as the second half of the fifth century. Three hundred years later, it became the leading center of crafts and trade and the capital of the first Russian state — Kievan Rus.

75. Sunset above Kiev and the Dnieper. This great navigable river was the source of livelihood for many generations of Ukrainians, irrigating the fertile plain and allowing speedy water transport north and south. At the same time it provided a natural obstacle to enemies from the east (pp. 142—143).

76. The monument in Kiev to Bogdan Khelmnitzki, a celebrated national hero, statesman and Cossack army general, who realized that the interests of the Ukraine coincided with the aspirations of the Russians. In 1654 Russia and the Ukraine were united.

77—79. Kiev's Cathedral of St Sophia, the architectural symbol of the city on the Dnieper, was raised in the eleventh century. Since then it has been reconstructed, damaged in wars and rebuilt many times. Christianity was one of the decisive factors in the integration of Russian tribes and states, as well as the spiritual and cultural medium through which the Russians came into contact with the Byzantine, Greek and Roman heritages. For a while, Russia aspired to assume the leadership of Christendom.

80. According to legend, Kiev was
founded by the brothers Kiv, Shchek
and Khoriv. In this early manuscript
they are depicted at the moment of the
foundation of the city: ' . . . And they
made the city, and they named it, after
the eldest brother, Kiev.'

81.   Odessa's opera and ballet do not lag behind the Moscow Bolshoi, or the Leningrad Kirov. The opera house was raised in the second half of the last century in late Classical style. Some of the greatest artists, such as Chaliapin, Sabinov and others, performed on its stage. The ballet company, which has toured many European countries several times, also enjoys a high reputation. The interior of the opera house is richly ornamented with valuable friezes and reliefs.

82. *Scythian gold, detail. Housed in the Kiev-Pecherski Monastery.*

83. *The Kiev-Pecherski Monastery or Monastery of the Caves was founded in the mid-eleventh century and soon became a center of literacy and the arts. Above it rises a bell-tower of original architecture, 96 m high (p. 150).*

84

84. The medieval castles perched on steep cliffs in the Transcarpathian region are a reminder of turbulent past centuries. They also testify to the high level of architectural and engineering skill in those times.

85. Stone idols such as this can be found in the southern steppes of the Ukraine. Their orgins and purpose have yet to be discovered, but it is known that they date from the pre-Christian period when the population of these regions adopted pagan idols and carved their figures in stone or wood.

85

86—88. The Ukrainians have a great feeling for beauty. Their folk artifacts, gaily decorated with vivid color, tell us much about their bright and optimistic view of the world. These people, living for centuries in harmony with nature and themselves, put all their experience into their popular crafts and architecture. Their sunny nature has been immortalized in many short stories by Nikolai Gogol.

86

87

89. World War II veterans do not
forget the path which led them across
the Dnieper to the Danube and Elba
rivers. Every May 9 the survivors
gather to mark Victory Day and meet
their old comrades.

90. Grandfather and grandaughter.
Respect of their elders and love of the
young are traditional values on which
generations of Ukrainians were
brought up. Until quite recently most
of the village population lived in
extended families of the patriarchal
type.

91.   Askaniya-Nova is the name of a
unique wild-life reservation covering
some 27,500 acres. Established in
1898, this national park still protects
rare and endangered species, such as
the European buffalo (bison).

2

93

92. The vast expanses of steppe end in hills, which seem like real oases, rich in pastures and woods and with lush vegetation.

93. Strong winds sweeping across the open expanses turn the arms of the old mill.

Land of Legend
The Caucasus

T he true origin of the word Caucasus (Kavkaz) is not known. It may be connected with the Hitite 'kaz kaz', the name of a people who lived on the southern shore of the Black Sea in olden times. The Caucasus is first mentioned in the tragedy of the Greek dramatist Aeschylus, *Prometheus Bound.*

According to legend, it was in the Caucasus mountains that Prometheus was chained to a rock for daring to give to mankind what the gods had so jealously guarded — fire.

The Caucasus is a region of legends and tales. This, is understandable since this territory — between the Black, Azov and Caspian Seas — is one of the cradles of world civilization. A legend often retold in Armenia says that after the great flood, Noah's Ark came to rest on top of Mt Ararat. In Etchmiadzin, the traditional seat of the Supreme Catholicos of the Armenian Church, a piece of wood said to be a fragment of Noah's Ark has been preserved. A wooden stick, purportedly part of the spear with which a Roman soldier pierced Christ's side on the cross, is also treasured here.

The area of the Caucasus, which today comprises the Soviet Republics of Armenia, Georgia, Dagestan and Azerbaijan, as well as southern parts of the Russian federation, is inhabited by more than fifty peoples, whose ethnic diversity is illustrated by the fact that they speak languages belonging to three different groups: the Caucasian (or Ibero-Caucasian), Indo-European and Altaic, each represented by a number of sub-groups.

Armenia, the smallest republic in the Caucaus, is about the size of Belgium or Albania. It is truly a mountainous republic: the average altitude exceeds 1800 meters, and even its lowest parts are over 400 meters above sea level.

One of the oldest countries in the world, Armenia is represented among the six countries on a Babylonian map drawn in the shape of a star on a clay tablet. That Armenia is one of the cores of world civilization is borne out by archeological excavations in various areas of this Caucasian territory: at the foot of Mt Ararat, in Satana Dar, for example, primitive stone tools dating from the Paleolithic Age were discovered. Here, too, were found the remains of the oldest human settlement on the territory of the present-day Soviet Union, dating back to 600—400,000 BC.

Remains of bronze and iron tools have also come to light, and in a grave excavated in an area that was once part of the bed of Lake Savan (2000 meters above sea level), a wooden cart with large wheels was unearthed, one of the oldest means of transport discovered in the world.

The name Armenia is first mentioned in the Bisitun inscription dedicated to the Persian Emperor Darius I, carved in three languages on a rock near the town of Kermanshah in 520 BC. In old Persian and Elamite the country was

94. The Crimea, a large peninsula in the Black Sea, abounds in spectacular natural landscapes. The history of Crimean settlements and towns stretches back into the mists of time. The earliest trading posts and forts were raised by Greek seamen. Representatives of many ancient peoples lived on the shores of the Crimea — from the Phoenicians and Khazars to the Pechenegs and Byzantines. Many great battles were fought here during the Crimea's long history (pp. 158—159).

95. Ay-Petri is the highest peak of the Crimean mountain range, which stretches across the southern part of the peninsula. It is some 150 kilometers long and 50 wide.

called Armenia (Armina and Armanya), and in Assyrian, Urartu.

The Armenian Empire emerged in the sixth century BC on a territory which had formerly been several countries, the best known of them Urartu. Its rulers left written records which show that they warred a great deal, but also built forts, irrigation systems and bridges.

The kings of the Artaxiad and Zariadrid dynasties (190 BC to AD 1), who gathered Armenians around them and formed Greater Armenia, did much to consolidate and advance the ancient state. The most famous ruler of that period, Tigran the Great (95-55 BC), further expanded its territory, which now

Miniature from an Armenian Gospel, 12th c.

162

stretched from the Caspian to the Black and Mediterranean Seas. Armenia was at this time a powerful slave-owning state with a culture which can be compared to the Hellenic. According to the Roman historian Plutarch, in 56 BC Emperor Artavazdes II founded the first Armenian theater, which performed plays by Greek and Armenian dramatists.

Armenia was the first state in the world to adopt Christianity as its official religion, in 301. The Church became a powerful feudal organization, which helped strengthen the state government and preserve the national spirit, culture and language. Near the capital, Yerevan, is one of the oldest Christian churches in the world (4th c.).

The adoption of Christianity led to closer ties between Armenia and Rome, but also to conflicts with Persia. Finally, in the early fifth century, Rome and Persia divided up Armenia, the larger, eastern part coming under Persian rule. In the fourth century, when the Armenians were struggling for their survival, an important factor was the creation of the Armenian alphabet by Mesrop (Mashtotz), famous throughout Armenia to this day. The Treasury of Old Manuscripts in Yerevan, which bears the name of this great figure, houses the world's largest collection of ancient manuscripts, some 10,000 of them, followed by libraries in Jerusalem (4500) and Venice (4000).

Among the texts preserved there are several thousand doctors' prescriptions from the fourth century filled out in four languages — Armenian, Greek, Latin and Hebrew. Foreign conquerors, Persians, Turks and others, destroyed many ancient Armenian manuscripts, so that only a part of this invaluable cultural heritage has been preserved to the present day.

After Mashtotz a whole galaxy of authors, translators and historians appeared, among them Moses of Khoren, called the Herodotus of the Near East. His *History of Armenia*, also containing facts about the countries of Central Asia, has been translated into many languages.

A remarkable figure of this period was the famous mathematician, astronomer and geographer Anania Shirakatzi, who scientifically explained the eclipse of the Sun and Moon and proved that the Earth was round.

In the seventh century Armenia came under Arab rule, but freed itself again in the ninth. Life in the cities revived, trade and crafts flourished, and new cultural centers arose — Dvina, Kars, Nakhichevan and others. In the following centuries Armenia was conquered in turn by the Seljuk Turks, the Mongol Golden Horde and Egyptian Mamelukes (1375). This marked the end of the history of Armenia as an independent state in the Middle Ages.

From the seventeenth century on, Armenian culture developed mostly outside the country itself, which was divided between Turkey and Persia. The first Armenian printing works was founded in Venice, where the first Armenian printed book was published in 1512. The earliest geographical map in Armenian was produced in Amsterdam in 1694, while the first magazine in Armenian was published in Madras, India, in 1794. The Armenian poet Sayat-Nova (1713—1795) lived in Georgia and wrote in three languages — Armenian, Georgian and Azerbaijani. Even Armenian schools were founded abroad — in St Petersburg, Paris, Venice, Calcutta and other towns.

At that time, as before, literature and art were means of preserving the national identity. Popular bards, who like the French troubadours traveled the land and entertained the populace with stories, fairy tales and songs, were also very popular. The well known folk epic *David of Sasun* tells of the struggle of the Armenian people against Arab rule.

In the early nineteenth century part of eastern Armenia was annexed by Russia, and in 1827 the Russian army took Yerevan fortress. The western part, however, remained within the Ottoman Empire. The end of the nineteenth

"Christ's Nativity and the Adoration of the Magi", miniature from a Gospel from the treasury of Matenadaran.

and beginning of the twentieth centuries is remembered by the Armenian people for the genocide of their nation by the Turks. In 1894 several thousand Armenians were killed in Sasun and twenty-four of their villages destroyed. A further catastrophe occurred in 1915, when over a million Armenians died in the massacre.

Frequent wars, the struggle for survival and genocide have caused considerable oscillations in the size of the Armenian population, which was greatest in the Middle Ages — around seven million. Today it is estimated that there are some four million Armenians: two million in Armenia, about one million in other Soviet republics, and over a million in twenty countries around the globe (300,000 in the USA, 40,000 in Argentina, 150,000 in France, etc.).

On December 7, 1988, Armenia was stricken by one of the most terrible earthquakes in its history. In three cities and some fifty villages more than 60,000 people met their end, the largest number in Leninakhan, which suffered a similar disaster once before, in 1926.

Armenia lies in an area where earthquakes, including serious ones, are by no means unexpected. An Armenian legend says that the earth is wedged between the horns of a giant bull, so that it shakes each time the beast tosses its head.

The tragedy which struck many Armenian families — in one school alone, five hundred pupils were killed — was alleviated by extensive aid from the international community. Experts and rescue teams were sent to this republic from all over the planet — French gendarmes and firemen, Swiss specialized search units, Japanese construction experts, and many others. This great tragedy brought people closer together and proved that this little Caucasian republic is not at the end of the world.

Georgia — A discovery made at Idabno, in eastern Georgia, confirmed historians' theory that Transcaucasia was one of the cradles of human society. Remains of ape-like man found here in 1939, together with earlier finds from the Old Stone Age, proved that Georgia was one of the oldest settled regions in the world. The first Georgian state, the Colchian Empire, was formed in the sixth century BC along the shores of the Black Sea. Museums preserve silver coins from this period, the so-called Kolkhidkas, which were minted in Georgia.

The Colchian Empire was closely linked to Greece, mainly by trade. The legend of the Golden Fleece bears out that Greek seafarers came to the Georgian shores and then advanced further inland along the rivers.

The Old Georgian alphabet testifies to the antiquity of this civilization. The beginnings of literacy date back to the third century, during the reign of Emperor Parnavaz. Recent research has shown that this alphabet resembles east Aramaic script, from which many scripts of the East are derived. The earliest writing in Georgia is to be found on an inscription from the Judean desert (433 AD), while the oldest dated manuscript is from St Catherine's Monastery on Mt Sinai (864). The New Georgian alphabet was formed as late as 1709, when a printing house was established in Tbilisi. The first book in Georgian, however, was printed in Rome in 1629.

The adoption of Christianity in the first half of the fourth century (337) was an important step in the history of the Georgian people, helping to bring together their separate kingdoms and spread literacy. From this period date the oldest Georgian churches, which still stand in the hills of this highland republic. These are Sion Cathedral (478—493), the churches of Tsromi (626—634), Djvari (586—587) and Ilarion Samtaneli (1030), the Patriarchal Cathedral of Mtsket (1010—1029), and others.

In the twelfth and thirteenth centuries Georgia was one of the most powerful states in the Near East, its borders stretching as far as Iranian Azerbaijan. From this period date the first connections with Kievan Russia: artists from Georgia took part in the mosaic decoration of the main church of the Kievan Pecherski Monastery.

In the second half of the thirteenth century the Mongols invaded Georgia and were not driven out until the middle of the fourteenth, when the Georgian feudal state was consolidated. However, Timur's hordes' attacks continued until the fifteenth century. After eight Mongol onslaughts, the population of Georgia was halved.

In order to secure a powerful ally, in 1783 Georgians signed a 'Treaty of Friendship' with Russia, but in 1795 the Persian Shah attacked the country,

Miniature from an Armenian Gospel, 989.

captured Tbilisi and burnt it to the ground. Fearing further attacks, eastern Georgia became part of Russia in 1801.

Georgia is a country with a rich and ancient culture, created over several millennia. This great heritage is imbued with a distinctive national spirit and character that have earned it a place of its own among the world's civilizations.

The history of Georgia in early medieval times is a chronicle of incessant wars, first with Byzantium and Persia, then with the Arab conquerors, who took Georgia in the second half of the seventh century and held it for the next four hundred years.

Despite this, Georgian culture flourished in the Middle Ages. Churches which are still admired for their architectural skill were raised in various parts of the country, and new towns sprang up. Tbilisi with its strong fortress on the banks of the Kura river became the center of the country.

Georgian culture, despite Arab domination, remained immune to Islamic influences. Architecture, literature and painting reached their zenith in the eleventh and twelfth centuries when a powerful, centralized Georgian state was formed under Emperor David the Builder (1089—1125) and further strengthened under the famous Empress Tamara (1184—1213). Academies were founded at the monasteries of Gelati and Ikalto, and aided the strong resurgence of the national culture. In literature the humanist idea was born long before the appearance of Humanism in Western Europe. Towards the end of the twelfth century, the great Georgian poet Shotca Rustacveli composed his celebrated epic *The Man in the Panther's Skin*.

In the late twelfth and early thirteenth centuries, during Empress Tamara's reign, in the central province of eastern Georgia, Kartalinia, a large group of churches was raised (Ikorta, Betanya, Kvatakhevi, Pitareti), notable for the astonishing richness and fine workmanship of the façade decoration.

In Georgia, a mountainous country, builders were skilled from very early times in constructing churches in caves. One of these is the Uplistskihe Cave near Tbilisi, its history dating back to the second millennium BC. In antiquity it was turned into a great underground city. In the sixth century cave-monastery complexes were formed in the David-Garedza desert (Kakhetia). In contrast to these one-story buildings, at Vardziya, in southern Georgia, a monastery with several hundred cells was carved out of the rock. Some of the main chambers are decorated with frescoes from the thirteenth century.

Dagestan — When God created the world and populated the earth, according to a Dagestani legend, he was left with a handful of languages. Not knowing how to spread them out, he threw them onto the highest mountains. That was how Dagestan came in being.

This folklore anecdote is a reference to the fact that in tiny Dagestan (50,000 square kilometers and two million inhabitants) in the north Caucasus, there are over 30 peoples and different ethnic groups with their own languages. Almost every valley has its own language and every aul (mountain hamlet) its separate nation. The most numerous are the Avars, Russians, Darghins, Kumyks, Lezgians, Laks, Azarbaijans, Tabasarans, Chechens, Nogai, Rutuls, Aguls and Tats. Many of these nations are little known, even inside the Soviet Union. There are 29 languages in use in Dagestan and as many as 70 dialects.

Dagestan has been famous for its handwork and crafts since ancient times. Dagestani wool rugs, hand-woven in the traditional manner, are highly prized. Made in brilliant combinations of colors, they are woven in many of the mountain villages of this republic.

The men of Kubachi have been skilful metalworkers since the ninth

Miniature from a Georgian manuscript, 12th c.

century. In earlier times, they made chain-mail, swords, helmets and armor, but today this artistic craft is mostly confined to making gold and silver jewelry.

Another mountain village, Balkhar, inhabited by Laks, is famous for its pottery, and the settlements of Ansalta and Anda for their black cloaks made of homespun sheep's wool.

Azerbaijan is also called the 'pearl of the blue Caspian', but this name is better suited to the Azerbaijan of the past. Today petroleum is the true symbol of this southern republic, bordering on Iran and Turkey. Its capital Baku, with its many oil rigs for drilling deep into the seabed, has a long tradition of oil exploitation.

Baku, a town with a thousand-year history, may have taken its name from the Persian Bad Kyy, meaning 'town of winds'. Some believe the name originates from the old Bakan and Bagi tribes who inhabited the Apsheron peninsula, where the town is located, in the twelfth century BC. If there is still disagreement as to the origins of the city's name, there is no dispute about the fact that oil began to be exploited here as early as the seventh century, when it was raised in hide vessels from wells.

Today many deposits have become depleted and production is stagnating. This is hardly surprising in view of their lengthy exploitation. Oil was exported to the Near East from the twelfth to fifteenth centuries.

According to the Turkish travel chronicler Evliya Chelebi (mid-17th c.), oil from Baku brought the Shah great wealth. Chelebi mentions a revenue of 7000 tumans per annum, and that oil was exported to Persia, Turkey, India and other countries.

In olden times, a large part of present-day Azerbaijan and the southern part of Dagestan were fertile, thanks to an irrigation system. Travelers recorded that these lands were better irrigated than Babylon and Egypt, and that vines, pomegranates and almonds were grown. Craftsmen made far-famed articles from iron and copper, clay and glass, remains of which have been found in the course of archeological excavations.

In the second half of the fifteenth century, the Safawid dynasty of Persia ascended the throne. At the Shah's court, the Azerbaijan language was used for the first time in military and diplomatic communications. The *Ker Ogli* epic has been preserved from that period.

In the early nineteenth century, after the Russo-Persian war, Azarbaijan was divided between the two countries. This put an end to internal feudal unrest, railways began to be built, and the first pipeline was constructed (1897—1907) from Baku to Batumi on the Black Sea. With an annual production of eleven million tons of oil, in 1901 Azerbaijan provided half of the world's output of 'black gold'.

The old part of Baku, with its narrow streets descending to the sea, has retained its appearance of yore. In the time when Baku became a well known port (15th c.) a double ring of ramparts was raised around the old citadel with a deep moat. Within this a number of unique monuments have been preserved, among them the Syny-Kala Mosque (1078), the Kyz Kalasy (Virgin's) Tower (12th c.) and the palace of the Shirvan Shahs (15th c.).

According to legend, it was from the Virgin's Tower, beside the southern walls of the fortress, that Shirvan Shah's mistress threw herself into the Caspian Sea on discovering that he was, in fact, her father. This tale has served Azerbaijan's artists as the inspiration for novels, poems and even a modern ballet.

96.   *The Caucasus, according to legend, was the mountain to which Hephestus chained Prometheus. Could the fire stolen by the hero from the gods to give to men have come from this long-extinguished volcanic crater in the central part of the massif?*

97.   *Armenia is sometimes called 'land of stone'. Inscriptions in ancient languages can often be found on rocks, carved in cuneiform or Armenian script. Armenian civilization is very old: the remains of the earliest known settlement on the territory of the Soviet Union, dating back some 500,000 years, were discovered at the foot of Mt Ararat, one of the highest mountains in the world. The name itself, Armenia (Armina), is first mentioned in the Bisitun inscription of the Persian Emperor Darius, carved in rock, near the town of Kermanshah (pp. 170—171).*

113—114. *Causcasian peoples have long honored fire as a symbol of life. Judging by its ruins, the Fire Temple in Baku must have been magnificent.*

115. *A mountain village in Dagestan . . . In one such village was born the famous Dagestani poet, Rasul Gamzatov.*

116. *The inhabitants of the mountain town of Kubichi are known far and wide for their skill in metalworking, wood-carving, embroidery and the making and decorating of pottery. Such crafts are highly prized in these parts.*

117. *A mosque and minaret in a mountain village. These ancient stone buildings, dominating the surrounding area, are notable for the austere harmony of their lines.*

Oases in a Sea of Sand
Central Asia

When one flies over Soviet Central Asia, these five republics (Uzbekistan, Kirgizia, Tadzhikistan, Turkmenia and Kazakhstan) resemble a large rug, decorated with rivers and canals, green oases and white cotton-fields on a yellow foundation of sand dunes. This imaginary carpet is fringed, on all sides, by a rich pattern of mountains. In the south there are the Kapet Dag and the foothills of the Hindukush, in the east and southeast the upland taiga and mighty ridges of the Altai, Tien-shan and Pamirs. The highest peaks, which exceed 7000 meters, and their surrounding areas are covered with the virginal whiteness of eternal snow. Here, in the mountains of Soviet Central Asia, vast mineral wealth lies hidden, and here, too, are the sources of many rivers which on their way to the lowlands carry water, and with it life, to the desert regions.

The comparison with a carpet is not accidental. Of all the crafts practiced here over thousands of years, carpet-weaving is one of the oldest and the most highly valued. Carpets are an integral part of the life and work of village families, as essential requisite of traditions and folk customs. Marco Polo, traveling through these areas in the thirteenth century, said that 'here are made the finest and most beautiful carpets in the world'.

Carpet-weaving is not easy work. It takes many long months, sometimes years. Carpets were presented to honored guests, kings and rulers, were sold for gold, laid at the feet of victors. In these regions the ancient custom that a bride must bring to the bridegroom's house a carpet which she herself has woven is still maintained. Such a carpet has some several hundred thousand knots, as tightly compressed as though they were fused together. Every little knot is a tiny dot of a whole pattern which the weaver creates herself.

Carpets — kilims — are laid down on the earthen floors of the houses, and the shaggy ones, zhulhirski, hung on the walls as decoration. Among the most famous patterns is that which bears the name of Bukhara, a city which is a 'must' on all tourist itineraries through Soviet Central Asia.

The history of many parts of this region has been one long fight for water, a river or mountain stream. This was an incessant struggle for survival against the harsh nature, against the sand into which, over hundreds of thousands of years, even the highest mountains turn.

'He who rules water, rules life,' runs an old Uzbek proverb. Or, as the Turkmens say, 'Where water ends, life ends.'

'The hungry steppe' is the name of the great expanses of sand that stretch southward from Tashkent for seven hundred kilometers. Its very name tells of the life here without sufficient water. Over the last few decades, a network of canals has been built, and water brought from great distances. 'The hungry steppe' came alive, but not for long. The ever thirsty land, now soaked with water, has brought salt up from its depths, and started to kill the vegetation.

118. There are countless mountain hamlets like this one in the Caucasus. Like all mountain peoples, the Caucasians have a specific patriarchal-warrior code of behavior and morality, as if the view of the towering mountain peaks gives them self-confidence and strength.

***

Over the black sand of the Karakum, between the brownish-gray dunes of the Kazilkum desert, across the burning Priaral plain, herdsmen and traders drove their starving flocks from oasis to oasis, from one well to another, searching for water and a better life.

The armies of the Persian emperor Cyrus, the wild hordes of Genghis Khan and lame Timur (Tamerlane), the troops of Alexander of Macedonia, the cruel companies of Huns who swept down from the slopes of the Pamirs, and many others, all passed through Central Asia. But this region was also crossed by more peaceable travelers, wishing to reach the East from Europe. Through here passed the famous 'Silk Road', the most important link between European cities and China and Southeast Asia. Marco Polo, who himself traveled

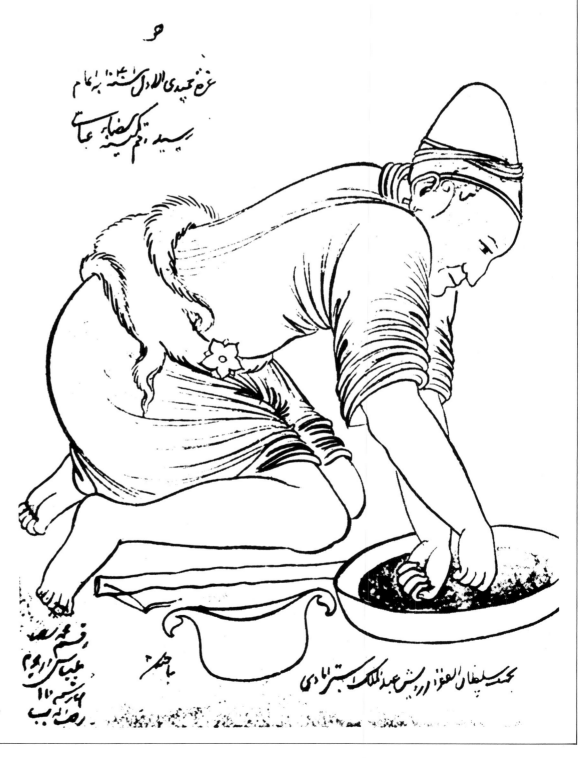

"Artist preparing his paints", miniature, 17th c.

this way, later described his impressions and was lavish in his praise of the wealth and beauty he encountered.

Among the wonders he came across was Samarkand, one of the oldest towns in the world, which has existed for over 2500 years. As was the case with other centers of world civilization — Babylon and Memphis, Athens and Rome, Alexandria and Constantinople — Samarkand was destined to survive many tumultuous events and upheavals.

Samarkand is in the ancient land of Uzbekistan, one of the cradles of world civilization. From ancient times, on its vast expanses, along the fertile valley of the Amu-Darya river, in the mountain valleys and on the steppe pastures, the destinies of various nations intermingled, their religions clashed and armies marched. The ancient inhabitants of these regions and their descendants, the Uzbeks, Tadzhiks, Turkmens, Kazakhs, Kirgiz and others, left their mark on world history.

The peoples and tribes who in the past inhabited Central Asia are first mentioned in the *Avesta*, the holy book of the old Persian religion, written in gold ink on parchment made of specially prepared hide. This unique book was written over hundreds of years, and its first chapters a thousand or more years ago. It is assumed that some of the authors of the holy book lived in Samarkand itself or in the vicinity.

The etymology of the name Samarkand has not been scientifically established. Some believe that it comes from the word 'Samar', supposedly the name of the founder or a conqueror of the city. Others suppose that the name derives from 'semizkent', meaning rich settlement.

However this may be, Samarkand has a particularly favorable geographical location, surrounded by abundant water, which is here called 'obi rahmat' — water of grace. Nearby flows the river Zarafshen, and not far off are mountains with plentiful game. Its position and some excavations have led scholars to claim that Samarkand is even more than twenty-five centuries old. The name Samarkand was first mentioned in writing in 329 BC in the diary of a participant in the campaign of Alexander the Great.

Since this first mention, many seem to have vied for the most poetic description of the town: it has been called the 'Heaven of the ancient East', the 'precious pearl of the Islamic world', 'Rome of the East', and similar. The history of the town is linked with names of many great poets and scientists, above all with Ulug-beg, today ranked by serious scientists together with Ptolemy, Galileo, Giordano Bruno or Copernicus.

Ulug-beg was a grandson of the great conqueror Timur, who took Samarkand in 1370. Modern historians describe Timur as 'courageous, cruel, a good organizer and talented military commander'. In his thirty-five years of rule he created an immense empire extending from the Volga to the Ganges in India, and from the Tien-shan to the Bosphorus. The richest lands of the East, among them India and Persia, were overrun and subdued, their largest cities razed to the ground. At the head of his troops Timur defeated the Golden Horde and burnt down the center of that Mongolian state — Sarai Berke. In the late fourteenth century (1397) Timur's army laid waste northern India, two years later it ravaged the Transcaucasus and Georgia, and in 1400 Timur made war on the Turkish Sultan in Asia Minor. In the battle of Angora (Ankara), in which both sides had 200,000 men, Timur defeated the Turks and captured Sultan Bayazit. After this, Egypt acknowledged his rule without conflict.

As well as a conqueror, Timur was a great builder. He wished Samarkand to outshine in beauty all other cities in the world. This may be why he named new settlements around Samarkand Misr (Cairo), Dimishk (Damascus), Baghdad, and similar.

Prince with his courtiers, miniature, 15th c.

Some magnificent buildings have survived from Timur's reign, among them the fabulous Shah-Zindeh mausoleum, the Bibi Khanum Mosque and the Gur Amir, Timur's tomb.

The last years of his life were passed in feverish preparations for a great campaign against China, but he died at its very beginning, in 1405.

Timur's grandson, Ulug-beg (1394—1449), was a ruler of a different type: he himself ranks among the greatest astronomers and mathematicians, and during his reign Samarkand became one of the world's leading centers of science.

"Architecture is also a chronicle of the world. It speaks even when songs and legends are silent," the famous Russian author Nikolai Gogol once wrote. These words might well have been written in Samarkand.

One of the most beautiful architectural ensembles in Samarkand is the Shah-Zindeh necropolis consisting of eleven mausoleums, built one after the other during the fourteenth and fifteenth centuries. Many consider that these unique tombs, each different, surpass all other buildings in Samarkand, even the famous Bibi Khanum Mosque, begun in 1399, after Timur's victorious Indian campaign. Having seen many wonders in India, he wanted his mosque to outdo them all. The most famous builders of the East were engaged, two hundred stonemasons were brought from Azerbaijan, and over five hundred craftsmen from India. Before its completion, however, Timur set out on another campaign.

When he returned, he saw the finished building of impressive dimensions (130 by 102 meters). However, he was dissatisfied and in his wrath ordered the builders to be thrown in chains.

A legend about the Bibi Khanum Mosque, preserved among the people to this day, gives a more romantic account of its construction.

It is said that the beautiful Bibi Khanum, Timur's wife, wishing to surprise and please her husband, commissioned the best builders in Samarkand to raise the mosque while he was away on one of his campaigns.

Bibi Khanum frequently visited the construction site and urged on the builders, but the main architect, enchanted with the beauty of the empress, was in no hurry.

When news came that Timur was on his way back, the architect set the empress a condition: the mosque would be ready on time if the empress gave him a kiss. Timur was almost at the city gates when the empress gave in. The young architect leaned over to kiss her, but Bibi Khanum tried to cover her face with her palm at the last moment. The kiss, however, was so passionate that its ardor passed through her palm and left its imprint on her face.

When Timur entered Samarkand he was astounded by the beauty of the new mosque, but, when he saw the mark of the kiss on his wife's face, he ordered the young man to be arrested and executed. Fleeing from his pursuers, the architect climbed to the top of the tallest minaret and when his pursuers followed, simply disappeared. He grew wings and flew to Meshad, the legend says.

Timur himself, his two sons and grandson Ulug-beg, are buried in the Gur Amir mausoleum. In 1941 archeologists opened the vault and found the remains of Timur and his no less famous grandson. Ulug-beg, whose life came to a tragic end on a pilgrimage to Mecca, had his head separated from his body. This seems to confirm the version of his death given in old manuscripts, according to which he was decapitated by his son.

Among the historic monuments of Samarkand, Ulug-Beg's observatory (1428—29) occupies a special place. Originally it was a round three-story building, forty meters across and no less than thirty meters high. The main hall held an enormous instrument for observing the Sun, Moon and other celestial bodies. In its time it was a unique building, with a gigantic protractor, sixty-three meters long. The main instrument, a sextant, was oriented with incredible precision along the line of the meridians, from south to north.

"Artist and Pupil", miniature, 18th c.

193

Ulug-beg is the author of the *Star Table*, an invaluable contribution to the development of astronomy. This book described the movements of the planets and contained tables recording the coordinates of 1018 stars. Ulug-beg also calculated very precisely the length of a stellar year as 365 days, ten minutes, eight seconds: he was out by less than a minute.

The *Star Table* was the highpoint of medieval astronomy, the peak of this science before the use of the telescope, which had not yet been discovered. The achievements of Ulug-beg's astronomical school had a strong influence on the development of the science in the West and East, especially in India and China.

After the great scientist's tragic end, the religious leaders who had prepared his death destroyed the observatory and the rich library, burnt manuscripts and dispersed his pupils. Fortunately one of them, Ali Kuschi, preserved a copy of the *Star Table* and published it.

The Registan Square, which in translation means 'sandy place', is the heart of old Samarkand. Once the forum and the trade and craft center of the city, it is enclosed on three sides by magnificent buildings. These are the Moslem colleges (madrasahs) of Ulug-beg (1417—1420), Shir-dar (1619—1636) and Tilla-kari (1647—1660).

Ulug-beg's college, in its time a center where Muslem priests gathered and were educated, had fifty rooms in which over one hundred students lived and worked. The building, subsequently damaged in an earthquake and set on fire during wars, was recently restored and now shines in all its former beauty.

The other two madrasahs — Shir-dar and Tilla-kari — are notable for their impressive size and magnificent ornamentation.

Close to Samarkand stands the ancient city of Bukhara, also older than Rome. During its long history, this city of old mosques, madrasahs and minarets was a real nursery of art and scientific thought. The famous encyclopedist Abu Ali Ibn-Sina, better known as Avicena, lived and worked in Bukhara.

There is an old proverb which says: 'I will give two bags of gold to see Khiva with at least one eye.' Of Khiva, another of the oldest towns in Central Asia, Arab geographers wrote with delight as far back as the tenth century. Like Samarkand and Bukhara, Khiva also has its history written in the stone of its unique architecture. The works of old master-builders, such as the inner city (Ichan Kale), and especially the mausoleum of Pahlavan Mahmud (a famous poet, but also a craftsman and invincible wrestler of the fourteenth century) are counted among the most beautiful architectural monuments of this region. Khiva, it is said, took its name from the Kheyvak well, whose waters have remained clear and cold for over 2500 years.

* * *

Each period leaves its traces. One of the most famous poets of the ancient East, Nuradin Abdulrahman Dzhamia, seeing the crumbling of what human hands had so painstakingly built, wrote:
"See the castles fall to ruins
The rulers have vanished in chains of wrath
No trace is left of their palaces
Only the poet's words live eternal."

Though many books were burnt and manuscripts destroyed, some works of the great poets and thinkers of Central Asia are treasured in libraries in Paris and Delhi, London and Washington, Tashkent and Moscow.

Many medieval codices were decorated with miniatures, as was the

Lion, drawing, 16th c.

custom in Central Asia. A manuscript required long, hard work, special knowledge and skill in calligraphy, talented copyists and gifted artists. For such codices the finest paper in the East, yellowish like ivory and equally smooth and durable, was made in Samarkand of the remains of silk thread after combing. This parchment was greatly prized by the artists of the European Renaissance as well, so that caravans carried parchment from Samarkand to Europe, along with other valuable goods in high demand.

The whole of Kirgizia, a small republic bordering on China, is over 500 meters above sea level. A third of its territory is over 3000 meters above sea level and includes the highest peak of the Tien-shan mountain massif — Victory peak (7439 meters). Almost 6600 square kilometers of the Kirgizian republic is under eternal snow and ice. At a height of over 1600 meters lies the large and famous lake Issyk-Kul (Warm Lake), 182 kilometers long, 58 kilometers wide, and in places over 700 meters deep.

Kazakhstan, on the other hand, is a republic of 'vast expanses'. It stretches 3000 kilometers from the lower Volga to the Altai, and 1600 kilometers from the western Siberian plain to the Tien-shan. Its total territory is 2.7 million square kilometers: France, Spain, Portugal, Italy, Greece, Sweden, Norway and Finland could all fit into it, but its population totals only 13 million. This is a land in which 'cruel Siberia and hot Central Asia meet', a region of mountain taiga and deserts. While in the south spring is in full bloom, the north is still bitterly cold and snowbound.

Like the Kirgiz, the Kazakhs were nomads for centuries, moving from place to place in search of fertile land. Mostly cattle-herders, they were often, throughout history, the prey of more powerful neighbors — the Tartars, Mongols and others. Only recently has their social transformation begun. New settlements are being built and the great mineral wealth has started to be exploited (iron, non-ferrous metals, oil, coal, etc.). All the republics of Soviet Central Asia today have universities and academies of science, a wide network of educational institutions, scientific research centers, large power plants and other industrial works and plants.

Baykonur, the place from which Soviet spaceships are launched and Yuri Gagarin, the first cosmonaut, journeyed into space, is located in Kazakhstan.

This is a rich republic. In the Sixties the steppes were conquered and today it is one of the granaries of the Soviet Union: over 60 million acres have been turned into arable land. The republic also has as many as 6000 localities where copper, lead, zinc, rare metals, coal and iron ore are mined.

Some fifty million people live in the five Soviet Central Asian republics. These are the areas with the highest birth rate in the Soviet Union; the republic of Tadzhikistan has one of the highest population growth rates in the world (almost three percent). It is quite common for a woman to have eight or more children. When her tenth child is born, the mother is given a medal, the Order of Mother Hero. The situation is similar in other Central Asian republics. A monument to the Mother Hero stands in the center of the capital of Uzbekistan, Tashkent. Unlike other Soviet republics, where natality is very low, in Soviet Central Asia the number of inhabitants doubles every twenty years.

119.   Through the blistering heat of the Karakum Desert, amid the brown-gray dunes, traders and herdsmen drove their bony animals from well to well, oasis to oasis. Many caravans laden with exotic merchandise crossed these vast expanses of sand.

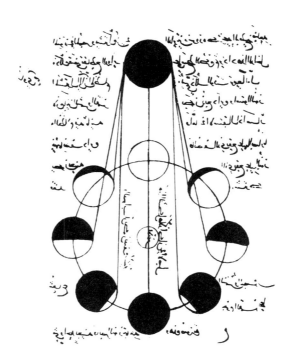

Phases of the Moon, drawing from a 10th-c. work on astronomy by Biruni.

120—121. One of the oldest and most fascinating ways of hunting — falconry. The hunters of Central Asia and Kazakhstan long ago learned to tame these proud birds and use their speed, fearlessness and deadly claws for their own ends. The prerequisites for falconry are often splendid artifacts, fashioned with the utmost care and artistry.

122. The Pamirs, the mountain massif at the triple frontier of the USSR, China and Afghanistan, with their many peaks of over 6,000 meters, are the dream of mountain-climbers. The sheer cliffs, impassable canyons and spectacular views attract expeditions from many countries (pp. 200—201).

123. Samarkand, the capital of the ancient land of Uzbekistan, is a cradle of ancient civilization. The etymology of 'Samarkand' is doubtful: some think the city got its name from a certain Samar who founded or conquered it. Many magnificent buildings, such as the mausoleum of Gur-Emir from the mid-fourteenth century, have been preserved here. This and a number of other edifices for which Samarkand is famous, were raised by the mighty ruler, military commander and conqueror, Timur the Great, better known in Europe as Tamerlane (202—203).

124. Fountain in Registan Square, in the center of Samarkand. Thanks to Tamerlane's ambition to turn his capital into a city which would outshine Baghdad and Damascus, today's inhabitants can proudly show visitors the unsurpassed architecture of its mosques, minarets, mausoleums and squares. Samarkand was built by the greatest artists and masons of the East, brought from India, Azerbaijan and Uzbekistan. Many legends are still told about the building of some of these edifices (pp. 204—205).

125—126.   Samarkand, Bukhara,
Khiva . . . it is hard to choose the most
beautiful of these ancient Uzbekistani
cities. The mosques and minarets,
schools and residences, with their
extraordinary ornaments, all bear
witness to the supreme craftsmanship
of their builders. Today these cities
have become great tourist attractions.

127.   Impressive architectural
monuments are found throughout
Turkmenistan. A special place among
them is held by the Great Kiz-Kala,
Virgin City, from the first millennium
BC, which was almost razed to the
ground by Genghis Khan's hordes
(pp. 208—209).

128.   The Kizilkum Desert. For miles
around all the eye can see is sand,
pebbles and the occasional rock
outcrop. Scarcely any plant or animal
life is found in these wastes, where the
temperature is often over 50 degrees
Centigrade (pp. 210—211).

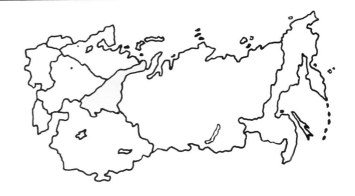

The Stone Frontier
The Urals

The Urals, the massive mountain range stretching for over 2000 kilometers from the North Sea to Kazakhstan, are known as the Stone Girdle of Russia. Actually, when the first Russians reached the Urals in the eleventh century, they named this vast territory Stone, while others, although more rarely, also called it the Girdle. The name Ural, possibly taken from the Bashkir language and resembling the word 'aral', meaning island, came into use at the turn of the sixteenth and seventeenth centuries.

The Urals truly resemble some great island lying between two oceans, the European and Asian, and form the natural frontier between these two continents.

The Bashkirs, one of the peoples living on the territory of the Urals, believed even in the thirteenth century in the myth of the warrior Ural who sacrificed his life for his people's happiness, whereupon the grateful people piled stones onto his grave, kurgan, forming the Ural Mountains.

As in all legends, here, too, hidden grains of truth lie buried. What is certain is that the Ural mountain system is a geologically old formation rich in various ores and especially precious stones. The famous Russian explorer Alexander Fersman wrote at the turn of the century that the Urals were a 'minerological heaven' on earth. In this belt, varying in width between 40 and 150 kilometers, 48 of the 55 most important ores exploited in the Soviet Union have been found.

Over 13,000 deposits have been located — from hard coal, iron ore and oil to gold, platinum and the unique Ural precious stones which have made this region famous. These are clear reddish-blue amethysts, smoke-colored topaz, famous emeralds, golden chrysolite, dark-red granite, greenish malachite, red alexandrite . . .

A folk story about the alexandrite, which changes color, says that in the evenings this stone shines like a bright red star for those in love, and in the morning, when lovers part, turns green with sadness and hides in the grass . . .

The Urals also yield a rhodonite of rare beauty with black veins and unusual color combinations, resembling some medieval miniature. As many as twelve kinds of marble have been discovered here, from the whitest, of the kind found in the Mediterranean region, to the black which is quarried in the Caucasus.

Many legends connected with the working of stone are still retold in the Urals. One of the best known is about the mason Daniel who carved a stone flower of extraordinary beauty. These legends, just like the secrets of the craft of stone-carving, were transmitted from father to son. The gem-cutters of the Urals likewise passed down their secrets, acquired through experience, to the next generation, but almost none of them ever rose out of anonymity.

129. Camels, 'desert ships', are still used as the main and most reliable means of transport in the deserts of Central Asia. Hardy and easy to keep, they also provide milk, and hair from which costly high-quality cloth is spun.

Even the name of the craftsman from the Urals who spent over five years carving a rhodonite cup that received a prize of honor at the World Exhibition in Vienna (1873) has remained unknown.

Today many masterpieces of stone-carving and gem-cutting by Ural craftsmen are kept in the Hermitage and other great museums. One Ural proverb runs: 'It is not gold that makes an object valuable, but good workmanship.'

A folk story tells how the emperor Croesus once took the wise Solomon to his treasury, wishing to impress him. But the wise man laughed and said: "All your immeasurable wealth is as nothing to a sharp sabre. Good metal, that is the treasure beyond price."

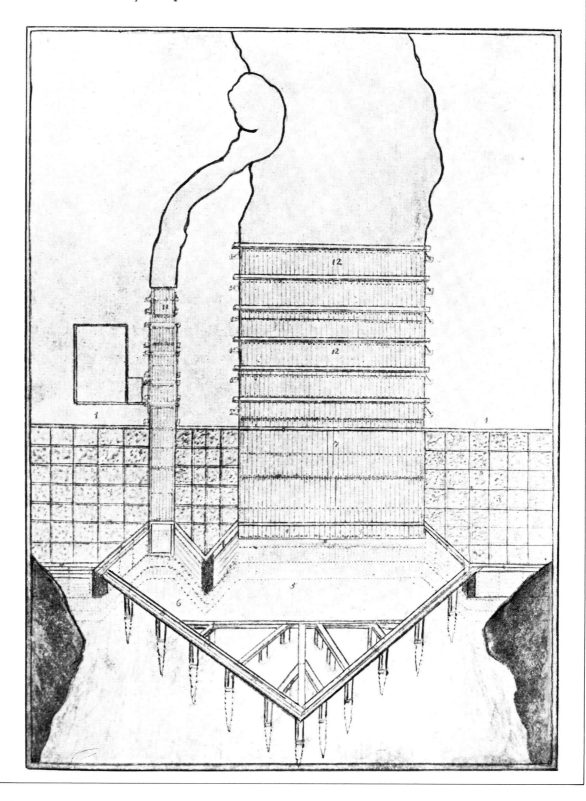

Wooden dam on the Ural river, old engraving.

214

Kosvinska gora in the Urals, old engraving.

In the Urals they still recall the sensation caused in Western Europe when the German scientist Alexander Humboldt reported: "The Russians have learned to make an excellent steel, 'bulat', and to forge it in the Urals..." 'Bulat' is the name for the finest steel used for making cutting weapons. In the Ural town of Zlatoust, the first 'bulat' was made in 1828. The forging of this steel was the culmination of a tradition going back many centuries. Long before the birth of Christ, the area was famed for its production of bronze and copper, and in the seventh century BC the Ural tribes possessed the technique of obtaining iron.

* * *

Many tribes lived on the territory of the Urals in olden times. Science even uses the term 'Ural race', which occupies the position between the European and Asian races. Its characteristics are dark, straight hair, medium skin pigmentation, slanting eyes and broad cheekbones.

Russians started to reach the Urals in the eleventh century, but did not establish settlements until the fifteenth. Following its defeat of the Kazan khanate in 1552, Russia incorporated extensive areas of Bashkiria and Udmutria, and Russian settlements such as Ufa, Sarapul and others were founded. This served as a springboard for further advances into the as yet unconquered regions of the Urals and beyond.

Industrial smelting of iron, copper and other ores started in the seventeenth century. The metal thus obtained was of high quality, and Russia started paying increasing attention to the Urals as a source of raw material. In the early eighteenth century the first factories were raised to meet the growing needs of the Russian Empire and its army, which under Peter the Great fought on various fronts.

The economic reforms of Peter the Great brought changes to the Urals. On his instructions, the quality of Ural ore was controlled in Tula's factories, with the result that 'the iron obtained for making arms does not lag behind the world standards'. Peter then ordered the building of the first iron and steel works, Nevyanska (1701), followed by Kamenska (1702) and a year later

РЕКА   ЛІВА В'ППЕРМІЯ

Yayva river in Perm, old engraving.

Yekaterinska and Jagoshinska. These first, imperial, factories were later joined by private enterprises.

The way to the Urals was thus finally open. Already in the first half of the eighteenth century, 63 metallurgical plants were built, and between 1850 and 1860 another 67, so that the Urals in a short time became Russia's leading industrial metalworking region. Alongside the factories rose cities: Yekaterinburg (today Sverdlovsk), Perm, and others. Yekaterinburg was built in 1723 in the very center of mineral wealth at the approaches to the Urals, on a river which allowed the transport of products down the Kama and Volga to the heart of Russia.

However, more people were needed for the recovery and exploitation of mineral ore, to build roads, prospect for gold, platinum and precious stones ... Qualified workers for smelting ore and turning it into metal were also in short supply. A number of specialists were transferred from Tula, near Moscow, but there were not enough of them. The uncrowned kings of the Urals, as the factory-owners were called, brought in new workers by twisting the law. They collected soldiers under threat of prison for some misdemeanor, deserters eager to escape military service, Old Believers and other sectarians who were avoiding exile, escaped convicts or peasants who had left the land. This strange mixture of human material gradually got used to the conditions of industrial work in factories. It was not surprising that Pugachov's army, during the peasant revolt of 1773—75, found most support and help in the Ural factories.

Soon other towns, Orenburg, Irbit, Nizhniy Tagil and others, sprang up in

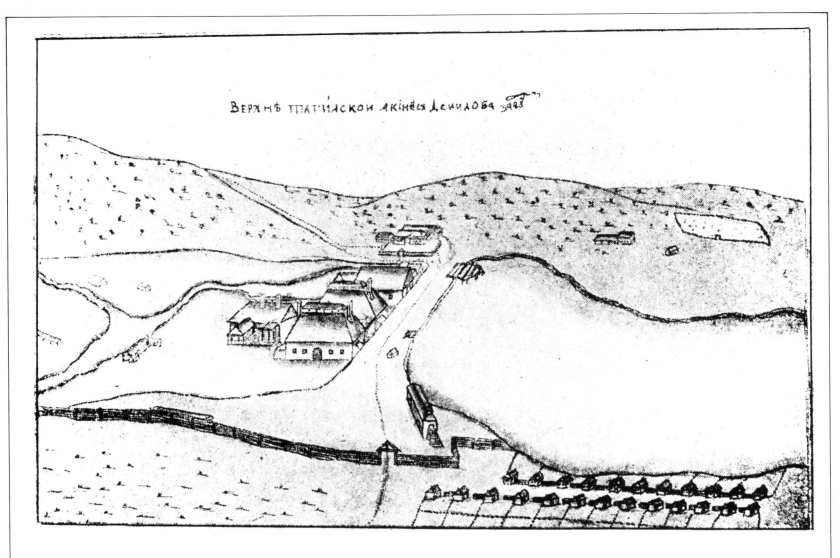

ВЕРХНЕ ТТАГИЛСКОИ АКІНФІА ДЕМИДОВА ЗАВД

The Demidov Works in Upper Tagil.

the Urals, and Ural metal started, for the first time, to be exported beyond the Russian frontiers, mostly to England.

At the end of the eighteenth and the beginning of the nineteenth centuries, a new tradition began forming: the forging of artistic wrought iron. Ural craftsmen learned this art in the Kamenska, Kishtimska, Kshvinska and other factories, and Ural wrought iron began to be used for the decoration of Moscow and, above all, St Petersburg.

* * *

Today it is difficult to imagine Leningrad without its many iron railings, balustrades, artistically ornamented gates, lamp-posts and, especially, the characteristic railings along the banks of the Neva and the canals. They have become an integral part of the city's architecture. Some 150 years ago the skilled Ural craftsmen forged ornaments unequalled in Russia.

In the mid-nineteenth century the Kaslin factory, where Nikita Teplyakov worked, became a center of iron-forging and the making of artistic figures. In the hands of this craftsman, it is said, an iron bar became docile and bent 'as though made of wax'. Old craftsmen claimed that Teplyakov could 'speak to the iron, and it listens to him'. Teplyakov truly enjoyed great respect, and the iron sculptures he made received international prizes.

The noted sculptors Lanser and Klodt, the creator of the famous horses on the Anichka bridge in St Petersburg, worked in the Kaslin factory for a while. These four life-size horses, placed on four parts of the bridge, were cast in bronze in 1830.

Rolling machine in the Old Ural Works, book illustration.

The Kaslin workers were entrusted with the construction of the Iron Pavillion which was awarded the highest prize at the 1900 World Exhibition in Paris. With astonishing skill, the Ural craftsmen created the world of popular imagination in iron: fantastic fishes floated in front of the visitors, ancient ships sailed across stormy seas and iron flowers blossomed.

The old tradition of the artitic decoration of weapons, mostly daggers and swords, was not forgotten either. In Zlatoust a factory was raised for the manufacture of such arms using steel made according to the techniques of old craftsmen. The ornamentation of these weapons, Zlatoust damascening on steel, became world famous.

* * *

Artistic metalworking is naturally only one part of the activities of Ural artisans. The production of iron, steel, copper and other metals was more important. Not without reason were the Urals called Russia's 'secure hinterland', its pillar of strength. This became apparent during Peter the Great's reign, when Russia was only just learning to stand on its own feet and when the first industrial enterprises were being built, but also in later times. Although after the October Revolution the industrial production of the Urals declined to only twelve percent of its volume in 1918, gigantic metallurgical plants were soon built, such as Magnitogorsk (1932), the Ural Institute of

Heavy Engineering, Chelyabin tractor factory, etc. During the Second World War the Urals became the main arsenal of the USSR. In the first five months of the war, almost 700 industrial plants in the European part of the Soviet Union were dismantled and rebuilt here. The Ural factories turned out half the country's steel and 62 percent of its pig iron.

In the course of the war, the Chelyabin factory built over 100,000 tanks, the most famous of which was the T-34, whose armor-plating was said to be impenetrable.

* * *

Wood, as well as steel, has played an important role in the life and economy of the Urals. The forested mountains (the highest peak of the Urals is 1895 meters) provided inexhaustible supplies of raw material for the production of charcoal, necessary for iron-making, and for building. In the climatic conditions prevailing here — long, hard winters and hot summers — wood was a highly suitable material.

When building their solid, strong, wooden homes, 'everlasting' as they say, the Ural inhabitants worked only with an axe, never using saws. Wood-cutters claimed that saws left 'open pores like wounds' in the wood, and that this 'speeded up the rotting and ruin' of timber. On the other hand, the axe 'covered cavities and in some way compressed them'. Surprisingly enough for the region which supplied the whole of Russia with iron, not a single nail was used in the construction of its dwellings. Ural craftsmen were famed for

Old smithy in the Urals, book illustration.

building houses, churches and even lookout towers without a scrap of metal. They claimed that iron was unsafe, since in time it would rust and turn to dust, whereas skilfully hewn and fitted wood could remain unchanged for hundreds of years. They were right.

* * *

The harsh climate led to the development of a special building style in the Urals.

Most often the whole house and courtyard are under a single roof. The window shutters are solid, with a strong bolt which closes them from the inside against wind or snow. The fences are high wooden walls without apertures. Into a large window a little one, a 'fortochka', was fitted. It was open winter and summer, not only so that fresh air could enter the house, but also so that bread and a piece of bacon could be hung from it. This was intended for convicts fleeing from Siberia and making their way towards Central Russia.

Master carpenters made the buildings not only strong and warm, but also pretty and pleasing to the eye. The wooden eaves, the frames of windows and doors, the weathervanes, all were adorned with lacelike carving. Particular care was paid to decorating objects for everyday use: spoons, plates, ladles, spinning wheels, children's prams, well-heads and so on. Most often they were ornamented with motifs and scenes from folk tales and legends, the fantastic world of wizards, animals and nature.

The most famous wooden sculptures were produced around the Kama river. Kama or Perm sculpture, as it is also called, flourished particularly between the seventeenth and nineteenth centuries, although it was mentioned much earlier, in the *Life of Stephen of Perm*, the Orthodox saint who brought Christianity to the lands around the Kama river in the fifteenth century. In technique and expressiveness it has been compared with the famous relief in a church in Krakow (Poland). Perm sculpture in essence has preserved the traditional iconography. It takes as its subjects figures well known to the people, such as St Paraskeva, the patron of agriculture and the hearth in the Urals, or Nikolai Mozhayski, the protector of new settlements, crafts and other skills. Linden and pine, less frequently birch, are used for these wooden sculptures, which are then decorated with 'levkas' (a mixture of alabaster and chalk), tempera, gilding, etc. Many such statues are kept in churches, monasteries or chapels, to which the craftsmen presented them so that they could be seen by a larger number of people.

130. The Urals, dividing Europe and Asia, are inhabited by indigenous peoples, today in the minority, and Russians, who started settling here in the fifteenth century. Their dwellings were mainly built of logs, since timber was plentiful. The spirit of the pioneer settlers can still be felt in the villages.

131

131—133. The Urals stretch south from the Arctic Circle for over 2000 km. Illustrated is a typical Russian village in the foothills. Life in these regions is not easy, but the exceptional beauty and variety of nature and the constant challenge it offers serve to compensate and motivate the hardworking inhabitants. In the virgin wilderness, hunters on skis can count on a good catch. The symbol of the Urals, and of Russia itself, is the brown bear.

132

133

134. Deciduous forests,
predominantly birch, cover the Ural
uplands. Although this region, famed
for its enormous mineral and other
natural resources, has long been
industrialized and exploited, vast
areas of wilderness still withstand the
onslaught of machines, pollution and
urbanization.

135. The rich folk culture is preserved in all Ural villages. The people here have a happy and open nature, and love to sing and dance. Almost every village has a folk music ensemble attached to the local cultural center.

136.   Old masters created their own unique style. Sculptures of the so-called 'Perma School' are compared, by some, to the best works of expressionist sculptors.

137.   Only the inexhaustible fantasy of Nature could have created these famous 'Ural pillars' in the central part of the range.

The Power and Beauty of the Taiga and Tundra
Siberia

At the end of the fifteenth century, notions of the 'eastern lands' were vague and colored by the fantastic stories of the rare travelers and merchants bold enough to venture beyond the Urals and lucky enough to return. For the Urals were not so much a political frontier as a geographical barrier which, during the long winter months, was almost impassable.

But the rich cargoes of valuable furs, gold and jewels which occasionally arrived from Siberia, and the tales of fabulous golden hills, endless forests and rivers teeming with fish, not only inspired adventurers and merchants to undertake the perilous journey, but prompted the Russian state to organize exploration, trade and military expeditions to the east.

Rumors of 'fabulously rich mountains of pure gold' also spread to other countries. When foreign ships attempted to reach Siberia by the Arctic passage, Muscovy became worried and in 1619 an imperial decree was issued: ". . . All coastal towns are forbidden to show merchants the way to the riches of the Far North, Mangazey; transgressors and traitors will be punished for their crime by a terrible death, and their houses razed to the foundations."

The 'Arctic passage' to the Siberian riches was anything but easy. It was only the 'tuska kocha' — the first single-deck Arctic ship built of the hardest wood — which eventually managed to drop anchor off the coast of the Kara Sea. These twenty-meter-long vessels with oars and sails were exceptionally suitable for such voyages and carried the Russians as far as the estuaries of the Ob and Yenisei which, together with the Lena, are the longest Siberian rivers.

During the sixteenth century virtually the whole of western Siberia was won and its peoples, the Samoyeds, Ostyaks and Tartars, subdued. The most famous conqueror of Siberia at that time was the Cossack hetman Yermak, who led his troops to victory over the Tartar Khan Kuchun and captured his capital Kashlik (1584).

Siberian towns are of relatively recent date. Most of them originated from little forts raised on favorable sites, mostly on high banks of Siberian rivers. The oldest settlement, Tyumen, recently celebrated its four hundredth anniversary.

Only sixty years after Yermak's Cossacks, having scaled the Urals, first laid eyes on the vast Siberian wastes of the taiga, Russian expeditions had already reached the shores of the Pacific. Dispersed thousands of kilometers apart, fortified towns sprang up — Tomsk, Turukhansk, Kuznetsk, Krasnoyarsk, Yakutsk, Verkhoyansk, Nizhnekolimsk . . .

These were, at the same time, bases for further exploration. The Russians soon adapted to the harsh conditions: the lure of new lands and riches was too great to be lightly relinquished. Many expeditions were formed of former

138. In the north Ural regions, as everywhere else in the Arctic Circle, reindeer sleighs are the most reliable and often only means of transport. Raising reindeer is a profitable occupation: herds of these small but hardy deer can be several thousand strong.

Лѣта ҂зрѕ посланы господа стопикаѯ василіи борисолѧѱ сынъ данпанъ масниѳи данпсатоѧоню ѣолопа данигочпиопъ стрѣля сты сапъ постаапша гра тѣлѣ и ѣла ѡъ пер. ҕфо чисыи слыи пѕурѣал ѡдикроша а сппиастиааѳо тпса псѣгѣ ѿстпгъ наѩ соипоѯиѧъ татарѣ собраша потѣрѣ ппотоѳла имсииѯ ппоииѯ.

230

convicts, social misfits or Old Believers, who left Russia after the reforms of Patriarch Nikon and the schism of the Orthodox Church in the seventeenth century. Descendants of these preservers of the 'Old Belief' can still be found among the inhabitants of the taiga.

In this manner great expanses of the taiga and tundra of eastern Asia came under Russian control. After the conquest of the southern belt of steppe around the Altai and Sayan encircling Lake Baikal, Siberia was finally incorporated in Russia. The new borders now stretched from the Kolina river in the east, and Cape Chelyuskin, the northernmost point of land of Siberia, to the southern edge of the Altai area.

Siberia is an immense territory: thirty-four Italys would fit into it, and still leave room to spare.

The natural boundaries within Siberia are marked by rivers. Western Siberia, stretching from the Urals to the Yenisei, is a predominantly marshy land, making the exploitation of its natural riches difficult. It is one of the greatest plains on the face of the earth, covering almost 3 million square kilometers.

Western Siberia is the richest area in the world in petroleum and natural gas. Exploitation of these reserves was undertaken first around Tyumen and then in the north, around Urengoy.

Central Siberia, between the Yenisei and Lena rivers, extends for 3000 kilometers from north to south, from the shores of the Arctic Ocean to the foot of the Eastern Sayans and the mountains around Lake Baikal. This region is mostly taiga, a word meaning ever-green forest (mostly yew, fir and Siberian pine).

"The power and enchantment of the taiga," wrote Anton Pavlovich Chekhov, "is not in its gigantic trees and total silence, but in that only migrating birds know where it ends . . ." And truly, breadth and expanse are felt in everything, leaving their mark on the character of the people as well. It is not without reason that Siberians say that 'one hundred kilometers is no distance,' that 'twenty degrees below zero is not cold' or that '40° proof vodka is not the real thing'.

Northeastern Siberia stretches from the lower course of the Lena towards the mountain ridges of the Pacific watershed on an area of over 1.5 million square kilometers. In climate one of the harshest areas, it was described in the past as 'damned by God'. Clouds of insects will descend on a deer carcass and leave nothing but a skeleton within a few hours.

In the far northeast lies the Yakut autonomous republic, covering over 3 million square kilometers, five and a half times the size of France and twelve times that of Great Britain. Yakut is almost as large as India, the second most populous country in the world, but is inhabited by scarcely one million people.

A great part of Yakut is in the Polar circle, and winter is here one long polar night. The Oymyakon 'cold belt', where 71° Celsius below zero was recorded in February 1892, is in the basin of the river Indigirka. In Yakutsk, the capital of Yakut, the winter temperature can drop to minus 60° in winter, and in summer rise to 38° Celsius above zero. Because of this enormous range of temperature and the fact that the permafrost is only a meter below the thin layer of soil, the houses in Yakut are raised above the ground on piles, as in Venice. The reason is that during the summer the upper layer of ice melts and this would bring down any building constructed directly on the ground. The depth of the layer of permanent ice below almost the whole of Yakut is more than 1500 meters. Rare specimens of animals and plants from prehistoric times have been preserved in the ice, as in a freezer. Several

Drawings on rock.

Collecting taxes. Drawing by S. Remizov, late 17th—early 18th c. (on the previous page).

mammoths ten to twenty thousand years old have been discovered in a remarkable state of preservation. An almost perfect example was found near the Berezovka stream, a tributary of the Kolima river, in 1901. The body of a rhinoceros, with its skin and fur covering, was discovered near Upper Vilyusk as far back as 1771.

Despite the permafrost, Yakut is a rich area. Its forests, covering over 300 million acres, have an estimated 11 billion cubic meters of standing timber, which is 15 percent of all wood reserves in the Soviet Union. Sable, ermine and other valuable furs, exported since earliest times, are still much sought after.

Petroglyphs, Murgur-Sergola, Yenisey river.

Yakut also has large quantities of something not found in other regions of the Soviet Union or most other countries in the world — diamonds.

Old legends and archeological finds show that diamonds were used as decoration 5000 years ago. The Russian name for diamonds is 'almaz', a word derived from the Arabic 'adamas', meaning invincible, unbreakable. The measure for diamonds, the carat, equal to one fifth of a gram, is also of ancient origin. The craft of cutting and polishing diamonds dates back almost 2000 years.

The story of the Yakut diamonds is a facinating one. Until the eighteenth century, this gem was mostly obtained from India. A number of individual stones have names and, according to some, their own curious and eventful histories.

The Shah diamond (88.7 carats), today kept in the Kremlin, is among those with a 'history'. It was found in India in 1591 and for over a century was owned by the Great Moghul. In 1739 it came into the possession of Shah Nadir who took it to Persia. This diamond came to Russia in 1829 as compensation for the murder of the author A. Griboyedov: the price of the diamond, in the

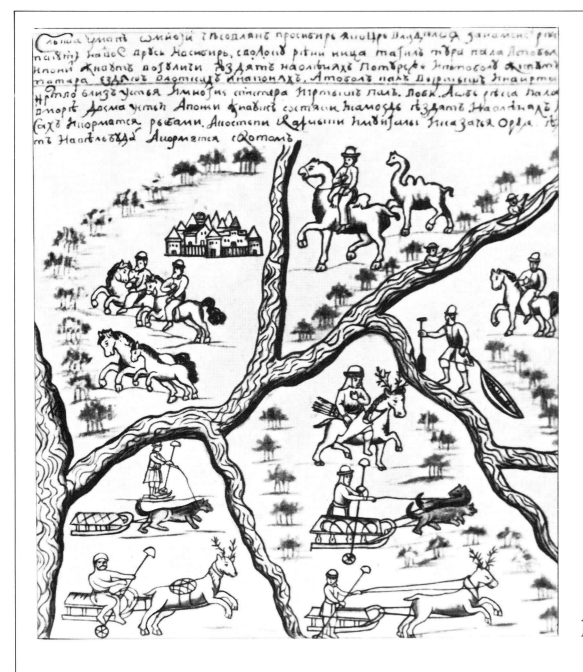

Means of transport in Siberia. Drawing from S. Remizov's chronicle.

opinion of the Persian court, 'paid' for the death of the distinguished Russian writer and diplomat Griboyedov, who was killed in Teheran.

The famous Orlov diamond weighed 400 carats when it was discovered in India. After cutting, the jewel weighs 194.8 carats. It is not known under what circumstances it reached St Petersburg, where the nobleman and adventurer Grigori Orlov presented it to Catherine II in 1773.

Until the beginning of the twentieth century diamonds were used exclusively for jewelry, but have since been used in various fields of industry, being the hardest material found in nature. Diamonds are still a 'hard currency' bought and sold throughout the world. According to a German professor, one man could carry diamonds worth ten million dollars, whereas gold to that value would weigh several tons.

Yakut owes its richness in diamonds to its geological structure. Diamond does not differ in its composition of elements from graphite. However, in physical characteristics the difference between the two is enormous. Whereas graphite simply adheres to harder metals, diamonds are a thousand times harder than flint and ten times harder than any manmade element.

According to scientists, diamonds were formed at a depth of 70—100 kilometers at a temperature of 1600—1700° Celsius and under great pressure (40—45,000 atmospheres), and then rapidly ejected to the surface in 'pipes' of Kimberlite rock, as the result of some kind of eruptive action — usually volcanic. If this 100-kilometer-long passage was gradual, the magma turned into the other modification of carbon — graphite.

Scientists in Yakut have discovered several deposits on the earth's surface and underground. In the richness of these diamond pipes, Yakut is comparable with South Africa. The earliest records of the discovery of diamonds in Yakut date from the 1920s, when local hunters came upon stones by chance. It is interesting, however, that organized prospecting for diamonds started only after the war. According to a study published by the Soviet scientist V. Sabolev, there is a geological similarity between the South African diamond platform and a part of eastern Siberia. Geologist G. Feinstein discovered the first diamond beside the Vilyuy river in 1949. Just five years later, dozens of diamondiferous areas were discovered here.

Pulling boats overland. Drawing by S. Remizov.

234

Gold is found in several dozen rivers and streams in Yakut. In the nineteenth century, many adventurers set out in search of gold-bearing sand. This proved to be a very lucrative occupation: between 1840 and 1850 Russia produced as much as 40 percent of the world's gold. In this period large finds were made on the upper course of the river Olemka and its tributary the Tungira. Since then, geologists have located a number of gold veins, the richest being around the river Tongo, a tributary of the Vilyuy, where the concentration is as high as 8 grams of gold per cubic meter of sand.

But the most precious jewel of Siberia is Lake Baikal. 'Famous sea, holy Baikal' runs a popular Russian folk song about this great lake in southeast Siberia which indeed is more like a sea, having an area of 31,500 square kilometers, a length of 635, and a width of 40—79 kilometers.

The lake contains one fifth of all drinking water on our planet, and more than 80 percent of the Soviet Union's resources.

While 336 rivers and streams flow into Baikal, only one flows out — the Angara, which later joins the Yenisei. The waters of Lake Baikal are so clear

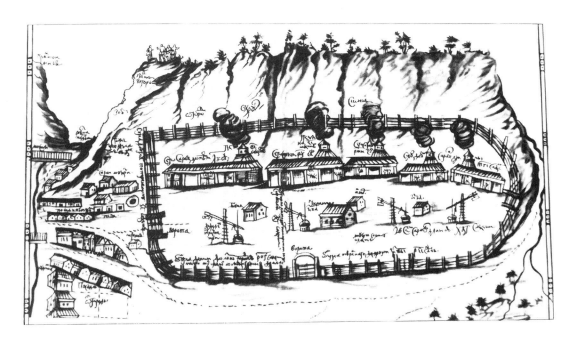

Old method of brick-making in Tobolsk. Drawing by S. Remizov, late 17th—early 18th c.

that its bed can be seen to a depth of 40 meters. Along its shores rise mountains that are extensions of the Sayans.

The vast expanse of water gives the area around Baikal its specific microclimate. The winters are not so severe, the summers cooler, than in other parts of Siberia on the same latitude. Lake Baikal is mostly tranquil, until local winds start blowing. Each of these has its own name: the 'barguzin' blows from the northeast, the 'kultuk' from the southwest, the 'angara' from the north, the 'verhovik' from the mountain-tops. These cause storms that can last several days, a sight both terrifying and magnificent, whipping up the tremendous quantity of water in the lake, which is 95 times greater than that of the Sea of Azov.

About fifty different species of fish live in the waters of the lake, the most famous being the Baikal salmon-trout. Lake Baikal is a popular tourist area in the Soviet Union, and the presence of many springs of medicinal water has led to the development of a series of spas.

The geographical center of Asia is located in the mountains near the

Mongolian border. The still insufficiently explored area called Tuva is surrounded by wide expanses of taiga, steppe and semi-desert. From Tuva to Moscow is 5000 kilometers. Its main link with the outside world is the highway called the Usinska Road. Here, in the mountain passes, it is almost always winter and blizzards rage incessantly against the columns of heavy trucks transporting cobalt and Tuva's excellent asbestos, exported to many countries throughout the world.

The indigenous people mostly live off the land, herding cattle, yaks, reindeer, horses and camels. They are also famed hunters and trappers: Tuva's furs, particularly sable and ermine, have always fetched high prices at European auctions.

In local folk songs this land is called a 'mountain glass with a golden bottom': the blue hills with their sharp ridges pointing heavenward seem like great glasses below which, in the bosom of the earth, precious metals lie hidden.

139. Siberia is so cold, the inhabitants say, that even the sun freezes. As late as the fifteenth century, Siberia was a great unknown for the Russians, who had only heard fantastic stories about its riches.

140. Most of the North Sea is permanently ice-bound. The Siberian shoreline is navigable for only a few summer months. As large areas of sea freeze over during the long winter, it is usually possible to take a short-cut across the ice from one end of a bay to the other (pp. 238—239.).

1

141.   In the polar regions eternal
silence reigns. There is scarcely any
vegetation here, apart from some
primitive, coldresistant plants. Animal
life is equally poor in variety. The
largest warm-blooded animals on land
are the polar deer, reindeer
(pp. 240—241).

142.   Raising reindeer is the traditional
occupation in northern Siberia.
Everything is utilized: the animal's
strength, hide, meat, and antlers, which
formerly served for making tools and
today are used for decorative objects
(pp. 242—243).

44

143.   This photograph captures the moment when the ice-breaker 'Russia' dropped anchor near the North Pole. A whole fleet of these mighty vessels patrols the North Sea, clearing a passage for other ships through the thick ice.

144.   The main means of transport within the Arctic Circle is the sleigh, drawn by either dogs or reindeer. This postman hurries with the mail, some of it perhaps from the sub-tropical areas of the Soviet Union.

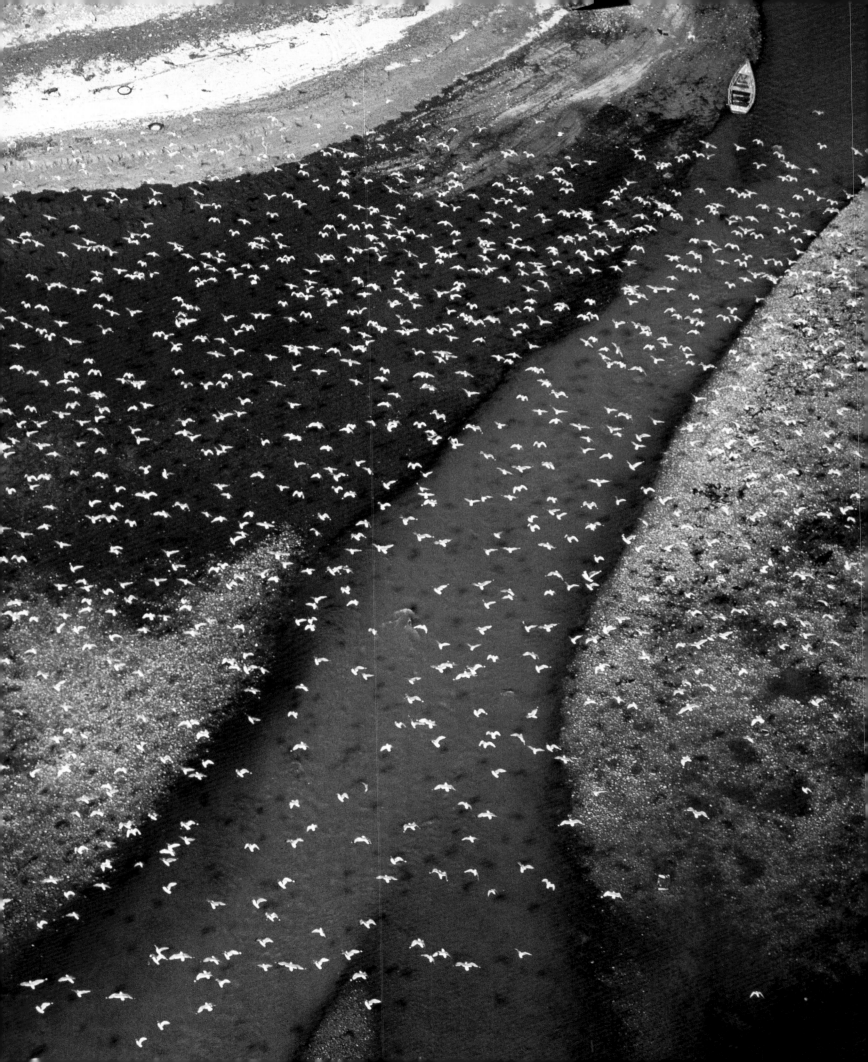

145—147.   Spring in Siberia comes suddenly and lasts but a short while. It is announced by innumerable flocks of birds returning from the south. The greatest Siberian rivers flow in the same direction — from south to north, and are navigable until the ice sets in the winter.

148.   The inhabitants of Siberia like to decorate their houses with wood-carvings and traditional patterns. The 'Sibiriaki', as they call themselves, the descendants of the early Russian settlers, have gradually developed a distinct character of their own and are respected as steady, resolute and fearless people. Their sturdy spirit and resourcefulness are put to the test every day in the battle against elemental forces (pp. 248—249).

147

149.   The Buryats, one of the indigenous Siberian peoples, cherish their customs and traditions, passed down from one generation to the next.

150.   A unique find — the tusk of a mammoth preserved in the frozen earth for several million years.

151.   The most costly and highly-prized furs come from Siberia, where long, severe winters 'clothe' the animals with thick, warm coats. Fur, a traditional Siberian export article, was often used instead of money as a means of payment in the past.

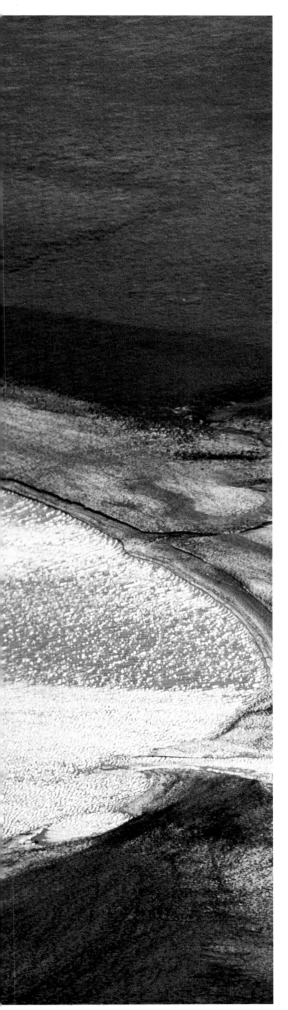

153

154

152—154.   For most of the year the tundra is under snow. This vast plain of northern Siberia has low, stunted vegetation and in summer is mostly carpeted by moss and lichen. Despite the hard conditions of life in this region, the tundra has long been inhabited by brave and hardy people — skilled hunters and fishermen.

155.   Nature in the north is cruel but magnificent, snow and ice its constant companions. Mountain ranges succeed one another, their peaks rounded by the force of the bitterly cold winds which frequently blow here (pp. 254—255).

156.   A bird's-eye view of the tundra in the spring. During the brief warmer months, nature awakens, offering the few travelers breathtaking vistas. The many rivers break their icy chains and continue on their way to the North Sea (pp. 256—257).

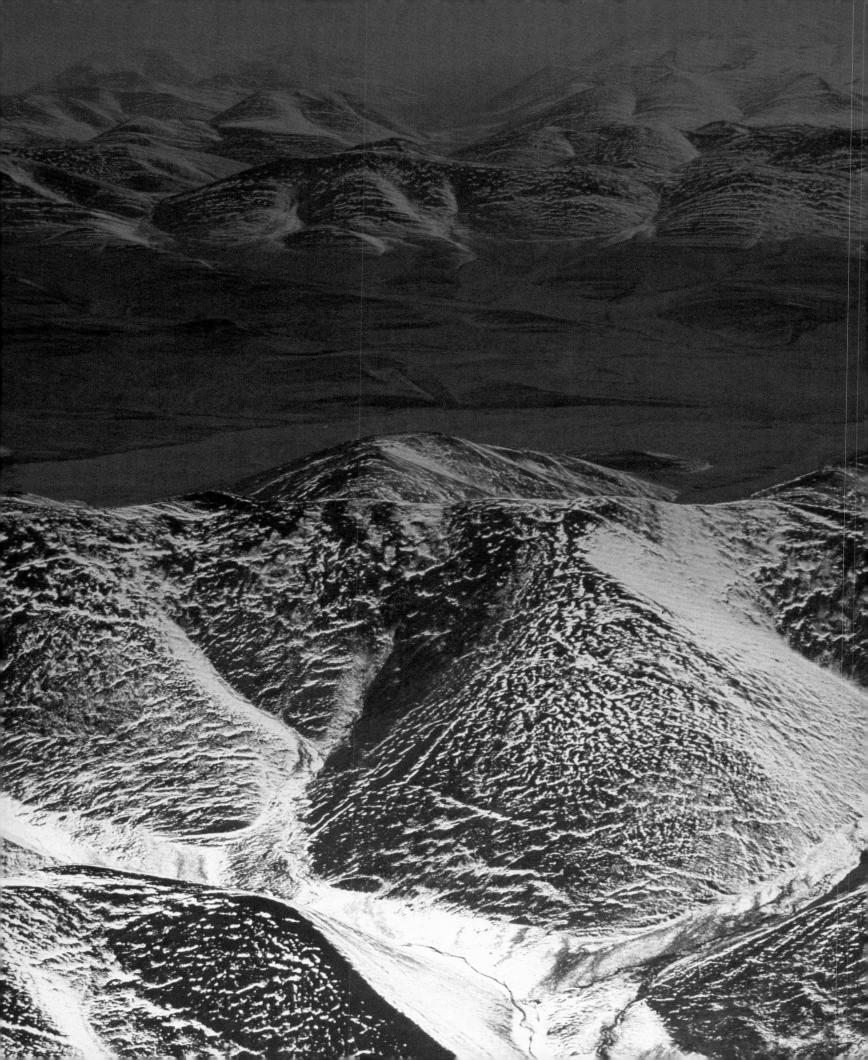

157.   A yak fight in the Tuva region: these two powerful beasts are battling for supremacy in the herd. Yaks are the main source of livelihood for the local inhabitants.

158.   The continental climate in Tuva enables farmers to grow wheat. This one is taking advantage of a warm sunny day to reap his harvest in the old way — with a scythe, a tool which has not yet been replaced here by modern combines.

159.   A special kind of 'medicinal' berry grown in Tuva is believed to improve the blood and circulation and speed up the healing of wounds.

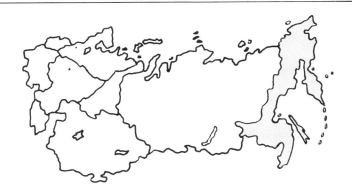

Chasing the Sun
The Far East

A flight to the Far East, even by the most modern plane, takes almost half a day from Moscow. This region is often said to be the 'eastern border stronghold' of Russia, the place where the greatest continent meets the greatest ocean of the world.

When a plane leaves Moscow for Vladivostok, Khabarovsk or some other far-eastern town, it seems to start chasing the sun as it flies to meet the day. Passengers can leave Moscow at dusk and not even see the night, thanks to the time difference: a full nine hours between the capital and the Far East. One is reminded of this time difference usually only by the New Year. While it is barely early afternoon in Moscow and preparations are being made for partying, in Vladivostok the New Year champagne has already been drunk.

Siberia and the Far East cover a truly vast area, over 12.7 million square kilometers, with a population of only 30 million. The far-eastern territory alone occupies 3 million square kilometers. Siberia is a particularly rich region of the Soviet Union; it is poor only in the number of inhabitants. The harsh conditions of life, climatic and others, are responsible for the low growth rate of the population, despite the material and other benefits offered settlers. The statistics sometimes show a larger number of people leaving than coming to Siberia. Towards the end of the nineteenth century, it had about 6 million inhabitants, and in 1926, 12 million. This is, however, a territory on which several hundred million people could live.

Today the Far East represents the largest economic region in the USSR and occupies almost a third of the country's territory. It is divided into the northern and southern parts: while the north is washed by the East Siberian and Chukotsk Seas, the southern part stretches along the border with China.

The earliest traces of human habitation in Siberia date back half a million years, as shown by finds from Upper Altai in the southwest and from the upper course of the Amur river in the northeast. Various cultures replaced one another in Siberia, starting with the Afanasievo (3—2000 BC), and the local inhabitants mingled with conquerors from the west and south. The first independent state in the Far East — Bohai (Tungusic-Manchurian) — was created in the eighth century, but already in the tenth it was destroyed in a conflict with Han tribes who had formed a new state called the Golden Empire (Chin).

The Russians started conquering Siberia after the Don Cossacks crossed the Urals in 1578 under Yermak Timofeyev, and by 1638 had reached the shores of the Sea of Okhotsk.

The Cossacks played a notable role in the conquest of Siberia and the Far East. In 1808 they were united in the Siberian Cossack Army, and somewhat later the Zabaikalska Cossack Army was also formed. The Cossacks were excellent soldiers and adapted to the severe climatic conditions.

160. Siberian rivers are famed for their great beauty and size: they are often several hundred meters wide. The Yenisey, Ob and Irtysh are the best-known Siberian rivers that rise in the south and flow northward. In the picture: the river Lena.

Early settlers building wooden houses.

The Siberian rivers greatly aided the further penetration into the polar regions of the Far East. The Cossack Semen Dezhnev passed along the Asian shore from the mouth of the Kolima to the mouth of the Anadir rivers and conquered the Far East. The Eastern Cape is named Dezhnev after him. He probably also discovered the land passage between Asia and America, but these discoveries remained unknown until the Dane Vitus Bering (1680—1741) established the existence of the passage between the two continents, later called the Bering Straits. This was in 1728, when he was sailing

under the flag of the Russian fleet for Peter the Great. Five years later he undertook another expedition, and in 1740, searching for Gamaland, sailed past the Aleutian islands and became the first person to reach Alaska from the west. On the return voyage Bering fell ill and died on an island near Kamchatka which today bears his name.

Explorations of Siberia and the Far East continued, and in 1742 Chelyuskin discovered the northernmost cape of Asia.

Shortly before the Second World War a Soviet expedition which landed with planes near the North Pole served as a reminder of the perilous conquest of the Far East. The expedition was rescued, with difficulty, from an iceberg off the eastern coast of Greenland. The members of the expedition were named Chelyuskins after their great predecessor.

One of the most famous Soviet explorers and conquerors was Yerofey Khabarov (born 1610), a Russian peasant and seaman. Khabarov sailed from Tobolsk to Mangazeya, as the territory of Yakut used to be known, in a small wooden ship and undertook many expeditions along the Amur river. He put together the *Drawings of the River Amur*, one of the first geographical maps of this region. Khabarovsk, one of the largest and most important far-eastern cities, an important military harbor and transit port, was named after this intrepid sailor.

An important step in the exploration of the Far East was made by the famous expedition to Kamchatka, a peninsula in the far northeast. These expeditions, led by Vitus Bering (1725—30) and Lieutenant Aleksei Chirikov (1733—34), established the contours of that part of the Far East, discovered the Aleutian and Komadorskie islands and answered the question of whether Asia and America were connected.

Navigator Aleksei Chirikov was Bering's deputy commander on his two expeditions and the first Russian to sail to the west coast of North America (1741). Bering sailed aboard the 'St Peter', Chirikov aboard the 'St Paul'. In their honor a town on Kamchatka was named Petropavlovsk.

The expedition of navigator and explorer Admiral Nevelyski established in 1849 the island position of Sakhalin and the possibility of reaching the sea by the Amur river. The conquest and exploration of the Far East progressed slowly and many great people made their contribution.

* * *

The vast expanses of the Chukot region, in the far northeast of the Soviet Union, are covered in tundra. The seas which surround this area on three sides are icebound for most of the year. Winter lasts eight to nine months here, and the temperatures are very low. The mean January temperature on the shores of the Bering Straits is 15—21° Celsius below zero, and inland between minus 27° and minus 39°. Minimal temperatures can be as low as minus 55°. The summer is short, cold and rainy, with a vegetation period of only 75 days. During this brief Polar summer the sun almost never sets, the earth wakes suddenly, plants grow fast, and the many lakes echo with bird-song. Following their powerful age-old instinct, wild geese and cranes fly here from the south. The shores are inhabited by polar bears, seals and walruses, and further inland live reindeer and polar foxes. As in Alaska, there is gold and tin in the Chukot region.

Only 12 percent of the population are northern peoples: Chukchi, Eskimos, Evenki and Yukagiri; the majority (70 percent) are Russian. The density of population is only 0.2 persons to a square kilometer.

At the estuary of the Anadir river stands the most distant town in Russia, Anadir, the administrative center of Chukot: 11,000 kilometers separate it from Moscow.

* * *

Until 1931 the Chukchi language, now spoken by some 12,000 people, had no written form. It was first transcribed in the Latin alphabet, and then in the Russian. Today there are writers who create their works in two languages: Chukchi and Russian. The most famous among them is Ritheu, author of the

Chukot Saga and the trilogy *Time of Melting Snow.*

The Chukchi and the Eskimos mostly fish and raise deer. They eat their meat raw and unsalted. During the long Polar nights, the men carve animal figures or hunting and folklore scenes, while the women make picturesque leather and fur garments.

Chukot carving is well known in the Soviet Union, the craftsmen of the village of Uelen being particularly famous. They are expert at carving walrus tusks, which can be up to 80 centimeters long. These are the most sought-after souvenirs in the Far East. The carvings often depict hunting scenes or walruses and whales.

In the clear, clean water of the Chukotsk Sea, gray and blue whales, fin whales and sperm whales can often be sighted.

* * *

The island of Vrangelya, with an area of over 1.8 million acres, epitomizes the nature of Arctic regions. It is a real 'maternity ward' for polar bears. She-bears come here in the middle of the harsh winter to have their cubs in dens hollowed out of the snow. The cubs are safe here, surrounded only by walrus, polar fox, white geese and gulls.

The island was named after Ferdinand Wrangel (1796—1870), Russian navigator, admiral and one of the founders of the geographical society in St Petersburg. Wrangel was the governor of the Russian settlement in Alaska for a while (1829—1835), and led many Polar expeditions.

* * *

Kamchatka, the large peninsula in the northeast, is one of the most pictu-resque regions of the Soviet Union. It is a land of volcanoes: there are 160, and 28 of them are active. High mountain ridges alternate with valleys in which geysers are a particular attraction. In the famous Geyser Valley, everything bubbles and boils as in a giant cauldron. There are also many mineral-water and thermal springs; the temperature of the latter can be as much as 100° Celsius.

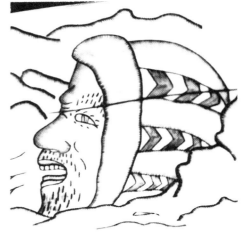

"Tale of a Giant", engraving on walrus tusk, Chukotka.

Kamchatka has the largest active volcano in Asia, Klyuchevaya Sopka (4850 meters), and the untamable Bezimeni, which hurls out fountains of lava and ash night and day.

Kamchatka, 1200 kilometers long and 450 wide, is also famous for sable-breeding. In the last century it was decided to establish reserves here for the sable and thus protect this rare and valued animal which gives excellent fur. Other rare fauna were also protected, such as the brown bear, the northern deer and the Pacific white-tailed hawk.

The indigenous population make up only some three percent of the inhabitants here, too. These are Koryaks, Itelmen, Evenki, Aleuts, and Chukchi.

* * *

Between the Sea of Okhotsk and the Pacific, between Japan and Kamchatka, lie the Kuril Islands, numbering over thirty, with a total area of 15.6 thousand square kilometers. Formerly in Japanese possession, they became part of the Soviet Union in 1945 by a decision of the Yalta Confer-ence.

Their climate influenced by warm sea currents, the Kuril have a lush vegetation (over 990 species of plants from birch to bamboo). Moreover, the islands have hot springs and warm lakes, the habitat of many animals and insects found in the tropical areas of East Asia. Of the 160 volcanoes on the Kuril Islands, 40 are still active.

* * *

Sakhalin is another hot-spring district in the Far East. The first explorers, enchanted by its natural wealth, named this the 'treasure island'. The Cossacks of I. Moskvitin were the first Europeans to see Sakhalin, in 1640. Some four thousand years ago it was inhabited by Tonchi, Ainihi, Nivhi, Evenki and other ancient tribes whose descendants are not numerous today.

For a while Japan and Russia ruled this island jointly (1855—1875). Towards the end of the nineteenth century, Sakhalin served as a place of exile for many convicts from Russia.

* * *

The main artery of the Far East is the Amur river (1585 kilometers), the largest in this part of Russia. In summer and fall it floods everything within dozens of kilometers around. The river is noted for its many different kinds of fish: 99 species live here, more than in any other river in the Soviet Union.

On the right bank of the Amur lies Khabarovsk, the most important industrial, cultural and scientific center of the region. It has institutes of the Academy of Science of the USSR, and schools for secondary and higher education with a total of 30,000 students. A large number of industrial enterprises, including a shipyard for sea and river vessels, are concentrated in the city. The population of the Khabarovsk region is mostly Russian and Ukrainian (about 90 percent), with a very few (only 1.5 percent) of the northern peoples — Nanici, Evenki, Ulychi, Nivhi, Orochi, Udegeiks, Negidals and others.

Jews (1.4 percent of the total population) have their own autonomous district in the Khabarovsk area — Birobidzhan.

* * *

The far-eastern seas which break on the shores of the Soviet Union, Bering, Okhotsk and Japan, have many characteristics in common: they are all separated from the Pacific by high mountain-island barriers, although connected with it by many gulfs. Regardless of their different geographical positions, all these seas have cold water. It is only in the fall, the monsoon season, with taiphoons from tropical regions, that a large quantity of warmer water pours in here. The areas where cold and warm streams mingle are very rich in plankton, and thanks to this, the seas teem with fish. As regards quantity and variety of fish, the far-eastern seas surpass all others surrounding the Soviet Union.

Pacific salmon is particularly famous. These fish breed in the upper courses of Siberian rivers, and live and roam in the oceans, some even reaching as far as the shores of California. Apart from tasty smoked salmon, it also gives red caviar which is prepared and preserved in its own juice.

There are three main kinds of caviar (fish roe): from sturgeon-related fish, from salmon-type fish, and from smaller fish, such as perch and pike.

Salmon caviar, taken from live fish, is first soaked in salt water. Oil, glycerine and sometimes antiseptic matter for conservation are then added. Fish roe, or 'ikra' as Russians call it, is rich in protein, fat and vitamins and surpasses many foods, including fish itself, in calorific value.

Most of the world salmon catch is in the Far East. Many fish farms along the rivers of the region look after their breeding and growth.

Pacific Ocean waters are also rich in whales, and lonely islands and capes are a haven for colonies of walrus, seals, sea lions. Some islands also have animals with valuable fur: sea cats. They come in groups every summer to their usual breeding places in the Komadorskie and Kuril archipelagos, even as far as the lonely island of Tulyan in the Okhotsk Sea. Here they breed, and raise their young, returning to the southern seas before the winter.

In the Far East many other type of fish are caught, such as cod, flounder, sole and herring. The Kamchatka sea crab, whose tinned meat is highly valued throughout the world, is bred on special farms. Modern fish factories supply the market with various other sea delicacies, such as oysters, shrimps, etc.

* * *

All three far-eastern seas are 'frontier regions'. The western coasts of the Bering Sea and Sea of Japan belong to the Soviet Union, while their waves break on the shore of Alaska and Japan to the east.

The Alaskan peninsula was visited by Russian sailors and merchants in the seventeenth and eighteenth centuries. In the second half of the eighteenth century alone, Russia organized some eighty expeditions to Alaska, and in 1784 founded its first settlement there. In 1799 Russian merchants founded the Russo-American Company, which obtained the monopoly of ore exploitation on the northwestern coast of America, from the 55th parallel to the Bering Sea. This company had the right of conquering territory which had not until then been claimed by other countries.

Russian government of Alaska lasted for about fifty years. During the Crimean War (1853—56) Russia was forced to give up its Alaskan territory, having insufficient military strength to defend it. The imperial government decided to sell Alaska, and of the two interested parties, the USA and Britain, chose the former. According to the 1867 agreement, the USA purchased it for the sum of 7.2 million dollars.

* * *

The largest town in the Far East is Vladivostok with over 550,000 inhabitants. This is the final stop of the Trans-Siberian railway and a large port on the Pacific. The town was founded in 1860 when Russian sailors landed on the shore of a deep, enclosed and very picturesque cove, later named the Golden Horn.

The Bay of Peter the Great, in which the Golden Horn cove is to be found, has the only Soviet marine reserve, established in order to protect sea and island flora and fauna. Located on the island of Popov, not far from Vladivostok, is the settlement of Stark, the center of the reserve, whose underwater world attracts particular attention. Here, around the reefs in the depths of the sea, live bright green algae (sometimes forming a wall up to two meters high) and sea cabbage (trailing fronds up to two meters long) as well as hundreds of other plants and rare sea creatures.

* * *

Returning from Japan to Moscow and observing the everyday life of Russian settlers in Siberia and the Far East, the writer I. Goncharov noted down: "And when a completely built up, populated and enlightened country, once dark and unknown, stands before a surprised humanity asking for its own name and rights, let history ask about those who built this edifice . . . These were the people who in one corner of the world raised their voices for the abolishment of black slavery, and in another taught Aleuts to live and pray and who, together, created Siberia, populated it and enlightened it . . ."

A century has passed since these lines were written. During this time great changes have come to pass in Siberia and the Far East. The distant land, separated by thousands of kilometers, not only from European but also from some Siberian towns, has ceased to be merely exotic or a supplier of raw materials. It has been turned into a region of developed industry and advanced culture, although this transformation is not, of course, by any means complete.

It could be said, nevertheless, that the Far East is becoming closer with each passing year . . .

"Tale of a Brave Fox", engraving on walrus tusk, Chukotka.

161.   Until 1931 the Chukchi language, now spoken by some 12,000 people, did not have a written form. The Chukchi are one of the many, but not numerous, indigenous peoples in the north which together make up only twelve per cent of the population of the Soviet Far East, the great majority being Russian settlers. This sparsely populated region has only one inhabitant per five square kilometers.

162.   The gigantic craters of volcanoes spewing molten lava and ash resemble scenes from ancient times, when the Earth's crust was still being formed. The largest number of active volcanoes are on Kamchatka and in the Kuril Islands. On these islands alone, 40 of the 160 volcanoes are still active (pp. 270—271).

164

163. Kamchatka is a peninsula of striking scenic contrasts, with towering mountain massifs and serene blue lakes, active volcanoes and peaceful bays. The famous expeditions led by Vitus Bering (1725—1730) and Aleksei Chirikov (1733—1734) played a major role in the exploration of the Far East. These two expeditions mapped the Kamchatka coastline, discovered the Aleutian and Komador Islands, and resolved the question of whether Asia and America were connected by land (pp. 272—273).

164. The coast is a true haven for many creatures. These gray walruses are called 'sea lions', though not because of their temperament. However, experienced people say it is unwise to disturb them when they are sleeping.

165. The rivers abound in fish, including salmon, much sought after for its flesh and roe, used for making caviar. The shores around Kamchatka, unpolluted and sparsely inhabited, provide a safe refuge for many rare species.

165

166. Here, too, the reindeer is man's best friend. The state farms annually raise several million of these beasts, which are allowed to roam the tundra in search of food.

167. The polar bear, the epitome of the Arctic, is under state protection: hunting is permitted only up to a certain limited quota each year.

168.　The waters of the far-eastern
seas that wash the shores of the Soviet
Union, Bering, Okhotsk and Japan, are
exceptionally cold, except in spring,
which brings warm southern currents
but also destructive taiphoons.

169. Reindeer breeders, a kind of polar cowboy, live in perfect harmony with the nature around them. Their material needs are modest, but they rightfully consider themselves the rulers of the great icy wastes.

170. Huge colonies of a type of cormorant (genus Phalacrocorax) find ample fish to satisfy their voracious appetite in the far eastern seas.

170

171—172.   Picturesque bays of the Okhotsk Sea. The reflections of sky and mountains in the calm waters heighten the impression of the magnificent power of nature. This was the magical attraction for explorers and settlers in the past. Today, these regions are inhabited by fishermen, hunters, geologists and seamen, self-reliant and dauntless men who brave the elemental forces.

172

173. Here, on the shores of the endless seas, starts each new day in the Soviet Union. The eastern part of the country has a nine-hour 'advantage' over the western areas.

174. Even to these remote far-eastern regions, civilization has brought its achievements. In these areas, where the traditional way of life is adapted to the harsh climate and centuries-long struggle to overcome ice and cold, motorized sleighs are a great help.

Chronology

"Jonah Disgorged from the Whale's Belly", miniature from the treasury of Matenadaran.

600—400,000 BC — Earliest traces of human life on the territory of the USSR. The Santani Dar settlement in Armenia.

8th c. BC — Kingdom of Urartu conquers large areas of present-day Soviet Central Asia.

6th c. BC — First Greek settlements on the shores of the Black Sea.

4th c. BC — Foundation of Samarkand.

4th—3rd c. BC — Creation of the Armenian Empire.

3rd c. BC — 3rd c. AD — Flourishing of the Scythian state in the Crimea.

1st c. AD — Foundation of Bukhara.

2nd—4th c. — Rise of Georgia, which around 330 adopts Christianity.

5th c. — Start of the great migrations of the old Slavs.

6th c. — First recorded mention of the Russians, who occupy the great Russian plain.

7th—10th — Flourishing of the Khazar state.

9th c. — Creation of the old Russian state, Kievan Rus.

882—912 — Reign of Prince Oleg in Kiev; the rise of Kievan Rus.

988 — Russia adopts Christianity as the state religion.

1024 — 'The Laws of Yaroslav the Wise', the oldest Russian legal code.

1122 — Reign of David IV (the Builder) in Georgia. Tbilisi becomes its capital.

1219—1221 — Genghis Khan conquers Central Asia.

1237 — Tartar-Mongol army, the 'Golden Horde', conquers Russian lands. Russian cities lose their independence.

1240 — Creation of the Lithuanian grand principality.

Stamp of the Ekaterinburg Mountain Prefecture.

1262 — Revolts against the Golden Horde in Rostov, Vladimir, Suzdal and Yaroslavl.

1325—1340 — Ivan I Kalita rules Muscovy. Rise of the Muscovite principality. Kalita assumes the title of Grand Prince.

1370—1405 — Timur (Tamerlane) the Great undertakes great campaigns of conquest and comes into conflict with the Golden Horde.

1380 — Battle of Kulikovo. Grand Prince Dmitri Donskoi (Demetrius of the Don) inflicts a crushing defeat on the Tartar-Mongol army.

1395 — Timur defeats and scatters the Golden Horde.

1480 — Russia formally freed from vassalage.

1462—1505 Ivan III (the Great) rules Muscovy, raises the Kremlin walls and builds churches.

1535—1584 — Reign of Ivan IV (the Terrible), from 1547 Tsar of all the Russias. Final unification of all Russian lands.

1584—1598 — Reign of Fyodor I, last of the line of Rurik.

1598—1605 — Reign of Boris Godunov.

1598 — Siberia incorporated in the Russian Empire.

1613 — Michael (Mikhail) Romanov proclaimed tsar.

1654 — Unification of Russia and the Ukraine under Hetman Bogdan Khmelnitzki.

1682—1725 — Reign of Peter I (the Great). Russia becomes a leading European power.

1703 — Foundation of St Petersburg.

1708 — Reform and modernization of the state administration.

1709 — Peter I defeats the Swedes at Poltava, consolidates the frontiers and secures a permanent outlet on the Baltic Sea.

1712 — Russian capital transferred to St Petersburg.

1721 — Proclamation of the Holy Synod as the supreme authority of the Russian Orthodox Church, instead of the Patriarchate.

1724 — Foundation of the St Petersburg Academy of Sciences.

1757 — Foundation of the Academy of Arts in St Petersburg.

Tsarskoe Selo Museum. Drawing by Alexander Pushkin.

Collecting taxes, engraving, 1633.

1762—1796 — Reign of Catherine II (the Great).

1773 — Peasant Rebellion led by Emilian Pugachov. Widespread internal unrest.

1799 — Birth of Alexander Pushkin (d. 1837).

1812 — Napoleon's Russian campaign. Battle of Borodino and occupation of Moscow.

1812—1814 — Liberation of Russia under the leadership of General Kutuzov, counter-offensive and occupation of Paris.

1817—1864 — Caucasian Wars. Russia occupies northwest Caucasia, Chechen and Daghestan.

1819 — Foundation of St Petersburg University.

1825 — 'December Conspiracy', an attempted coup d'etat by the liberal aristocracy (Dekabrists).

1825—1855 — Reign of Nicholas (Nikolai) I.

1828—1829 — Russo-Turkish War. Consolidation of the southern frontiers.

1828 — Birth of Leo (Lav) Tolstoi (d. 1910).

1834 — Birth of D. I. Mendeleyev, creator of the Periodic Table of chemical elements (d. 1907).

1853—1856 — Crimean War. Russia extends its frontier with Turkey.

1861 — Abolition of serfdom.

1881 — Alexander II assassinated by members of the revolutionary 'People's Will' organization.

1905 — Russo-Japanese War, in which Russia suffers defeat.

1914 — Germany declares war on Russia. Entry of Russia into the First World War.

1917 — February: bourgeois revolution and abolition of the monarchy. October: socialist revolution under the leadership of V. I. Lenin.

1918 — Russia withdraws from the First World War.

1924 — Death of Lenin. J. V. Stalin assumes power.

1940 — Soviet-Finnish War.

1941 — German attack on the USSR.

1942—1943 — Battle of Stalingrad. Red Army launches a counter-offensive.

1945 — Capitulation of Germany.

1961 — Yuri Gagarin becomes the first man in space.

Self-portrait of Alexander Pushkin.

287

NORWAY

SWEDEN

BALTIC SEA

FINLAND

ARCTIC O

POLAND

LITHUANIAN SSR

LATVIAN SSR

ESTONIAN SSR

Karelia

ROMANIA

BELORUSSIAN SSR

UKRAINIAN SSR

MOLDAVIAN SSR

Moscow

R U S S I A N

Komi

S O V I E T   F E D E R

CRIMEA

BLACK SEA

SEA OF AZOV

Mordvinia

Chuvasia

Marii

Udmurtia

Tataria

Bashkiria

Kalmikia

Abkhazia

Adzharia

GEORGIAN SSR

TURKEY

ARMENIAN SSR

Kabarda

North Ossetia

Checheno-Inghushia

Dagestan

AZERBAIJAN SSR

Nakhichevan

CASPIAN

SEA

KAZAKH SSR

ARAL SEA

Kara-Kalpakia

IRAN

TURKMEN SSR

UZBEK SSR

KIRGIZ SSR

TADZHIK SSR

AFGHANISTAN

CHINA